MW01234618

Interior Design by FormattedBooks

CONTENTS

INTRODUCTION

> If life gives you lemons, make lemonade.
> **—ELBERT HUBBARD**

There are two types of people in this world: those who live a sedentary life and are satisfied with the circumstances and conditions they are born in. While there are others, who aren't content with the way things are. Their thirst cannot be easily quenched. They want more from life and are willing to explore the beauty and adventure this world offers. They are hustlers and real change-makers who trek the unpredictable terrains of life with courage and resilience, making lemonade out of every challenge the world throws at them.

We are about to go down the storyline of one such person. A young girl who journeyed from the land of ancient pharaohs to the exotic neighborhoods of Libya and went hopping between cultures to finally arrive in the USA in 2000. She surfed through waves of cultural difference and embraced the new world with open arms. Where her roots lie in the ancient history of pyramids, her heart is in the USA.

She had carefully adorned her bicultural, or one would say a tri-cultural identity with a blend of Eastern and Western values and norms. Though the American culture shocked her, she resiliently overcame the barriers to finally have her own American way of life. She meticulously sewed her traditional roots with American modernity and resiliently charted her own path.

While she fiercely navigated the murky waters of cultural differences, she also had a tough time in her married life. Her first marriage, in 2006, was an unfortunate one. Though God blessed her with a beautiful daughter that she adores, the toxic nature of the relationship led to divorce, which is not easy to go about when children are involved. She remarried in 2020 when her daughter was just a teenager. There were many obstacles that kept coming in the way of the mother-daughter relationship, and they eventually overcame them all. Perhaps the daughter had her mother's gift: resilience. Like mother, like daughter. With each passing day, she was prouder than ever to see her daughter blossom into a confident and resilient individual.

The Egyptian girl-turned-woman navigated different cultures, languages, and dysfunctional relationships; she never lost hope. She adapted to the environment, remained steadfast, and raised a daughter she is really proud of.

That tri-cultural girl who is now a woman is me, Reham Sadek. I am a mother and a Psychiatrist who focuses on issues affecting children, adolescents, and adults. I am based in the USA, and above is an abridged version of a story that many immigrant parents in America might share.

Many of you would be wondering how I managed to raise a daughter who can turn any situation around, face any challenge, and make lemonade no matter what the world throws at her. The answer for me lies in parental care and support. The way we, as parents, tend to raise our children defines what they might become as adults. In my journey, I owe my resilience to the unwavering support of my parents, who supported me through thick and thin and still do to this day. Who knows how things would have been if it were not for them? The resilience they imbibed in me made it possible for me to transfer it to my daughter so that she can courageously live through the harsh realities of life.

In the world right now, there is a parenting crisis as society is changing quickly, and parents are having difficulties raising kids. Hence, as a psychiatrist and a parent, I felt this urge to intervene. This is why I am writing this book: to share the experiences and techniques I learned as a mother and psychiatry practitioner over the years. In this book, we aim to know what parenting needs are in these changing times and how, as parents, we can raise confident, unafraid, and resilient kids who can really squeeze the lemons of life.

THE TIME IN WHICH WE LIVE

The age in which we live today is nothing like it was when we were children and is unlike anything our forefathers witnessed. The world has gone through tremendous change and evolution. Where social media and technology have revolutionized business, they have also transformed the sense of self, values, culture, and relationships. Despite bringing so much ease and benefits, this new world has its shortcomings, and we all know this very well.

In this day and age, life is faster-paced than ever. The competition in the market is cutthroat. Young people all around seem to be in a rat race. Mental pressure and stress in this globalized digital age are paramount, not necessarily because of increasing divorce rates and dysfunctional families but also because of social expectations, social media, and workload. Our kids endure a lot more than previous generations when it comes to exams, jobs, work, or self-fulfillment.

In the midst of a culture where bullying, harassment, comparisons, and cybercrimes reign supreme and render our children victims of different complexes, we must help them through these murky waters of a toxic culture. As parents, we are both concerned and willing to help our children in a way that they can survive the pressures of this age.

By choosing to read this book, you have already embarked on the journey of helping your kids become resilient and steadfast. I congratulate you for taking a step in the right direction!

WHAT TO EXPECT

Through years of research and practice in psychiatry, I learned that grit and resilience are two significant predictors of future success. This conclusion, coupled with my personal experience, motivated me to write this book to share the knowledge with parents struggling to raise their children in these tumultuous times. As parents, it is our duty to equip our children with the tools and resources to help them have a bright future, and the first step in this direction is to ensure that they can handle any situation that life throws at them.

In this book, we will embark on a journey to explore misconceptions about the true meaning of resilience and how we, as parents, can foster that. We will also run through different practical strategies and resources in the process.

Whether you have gone through a similar situation as I have or something completely different; whether you are an over-protective dad or a mom; single-parent or a couple; or you are someone who wants to improve the parent-child dynamic; or someone who has moved to a new house or city with a family; or a parent who has immigrated with kids, this book is for you.

Some of the things that you can expect from this book are as follows:

- Practical strategies that will help your child become resilient
- Understanding a Growth Mindset—and how it helps children be more resilient.

- The 7 C's of Resilience, according to Dr. Ginsburg
- How to help children find the balance between self-reliance and knowing when to ask for help.
- The top 3 skills children need to help them build resilience.
- The positive relationship between resilience and self-care.
- The dangers of cyberbullying—and how resilience plays a protective role.

Our primary focus is 'resilience' and how parenting can foster it. Our kids need to be not only independent and confident but also fearless. Whether you have moved to a different country, relocated to another state, suffered through economic insolvency, or a disease has befallen a family member, whatever has happened, if you want your child to stand their ground no matter what, this is your call to action.

Follow me through each page and word; crawl over the sentences with vigorous curiosity and determination, and you will realize how you can affect change.

Truth be told, it's not easy. Nothing worth fighting for is ever easy. But let me tell you: Building resilience is absolutely worth it. It does not matter whether the schools close again, hell breaks, the heavens fall, a meteor strikes earth on this very day, a volcano erupts, or an economic crisis grips the nation; I know that my child and yours will stand tall against such odds.

I want you to embody the kind of confidence that the latter sentence contained. I want you to know that when you send your kids off to college or the workforce for the first time, they'll be alright without you.

ARE YOU READY?

1

DEFINING RESILIENCE

> The human capacity for burden is like bamboo—far more flexible than you'd ever believe at first glance.
>
> **—JODI PICOULT**

I n this chapter, we will dive into the spirit that great heroes and conquerors artfully honed. We will embark on an intellectual journey to understand a gift that all great people have exhibited throughout history. The gift that shielded them from life's arrows like armor, the gift that guided their mission like spirit, the gift that, like a lamp, shone hope in the depths of darkness. That gift is resilience. This chapter will bring forth the wisdom hidden in the concept of resilience, what it means for children, and how it differs from other qualities like persistence and resistance. It will also discuss why resilience matters.

WHAT IS RESILIENCE?

Resilience means the capacity to withstand or to recover quickly from difficulties. It refers to the ability to adapt to different situations and circumstances. It means the ability to handle tough times like a champion. However, it is easier said than done. This life is like a boxing ring where punches from all directions are thrown at us to knock us down and our little ones. This is what life is, the perpetual struggle against the odds.

In such difficult situations, accepting defeat and assuming the fetal position is more effortless. It is in this situation that resilience swoops in to save the day. You get up courageously, fight back, defend yourself against the punches life throws, and emerge victorious against all odds. This courage, this hope, and this ability to bounce back and never quit are the fruits of resilience.

Resilience is not just about winning and being tough in the face of adversity; it is an attitude and an entire way of thinking. Failure is a part of life. Your child may never get the first position or the highest grade in school or may have lost a sports game. It is not important whether they win or lose. They must be willing to stand up again, learn from their mistakes, and try again next time. As someone said, "You only lose when you quit."

A similar situation occurs with their schoolwork. Why expect them to excel in school when we keep nagging them about studying harder, as if life is all about academics? For a child's healthy development, extracurricular activities are as important as academics. We all want our children to get good grades and succeed in life, and we passionately want to motivate them. But we should be vigilant about approaching and encouraging our children, as we cannot snub or break their spirits for merely getting a C in an exam because there can be other more suitable ways of comforting and helping your child than forcing them to study more. This is just one example. It's critical to remember that a child's worth and potential are not solely determined by academic achievement. They can grow and develop more fully if you support them emotionally, encourage their interests, and create a positive learning environment. Instead of just concentrating on grades, our ultimate objective should be to foster well-rounded individuals driven by their passions and goals.

In light of resilience, let us briefly talk about endurance. We all want our children to have high endurance levels, but that does not mean they should continue enduring no matter what happens. Endurance is about tolerating the situation, whereas resilience is knowing when enough is enough. For example, mere endurance would do no good if a child is bullied at school. He must be resilient enough to say no when it's needed. Qualities like endurance and resilience can be modeled through the behaviors of parents. We are helping ourselves and doing a favor to our children when we stand up for ourselves. It is important to note that when we stay in abusive relationships and endure it, we send our children the wrong message of remaining silent when the going gets tough. After all, who wants their children to simply endure and suffer? We want them to be nothing less than resilient!

Resilience VS Resistance

Resistance versus resilience! It might sound interesting, right? Often conflated as the same thing, there is a slight difference between the two. They may seem similar, but they are not peas in the same pod. Where resilience is about facing challenging situations, resistance is about avoiding them. Resistance can be defined as "the refusal to accept or comply with something."

The main difference is that "resilience is all about overcoming challenges you face, and resistance is avoiding problems" (Jon, 2022b).

To put it plainly, for example, if your child is aspiring for a particular goal but is having trouble attaining it, there might be resistance coming his way. There may be avoidance of putting energies in the right direction. If you and your child have planned to get an A, but he is avoiding putting in the hard work; he is procrastinating and dodging the tasks, or you both have planned to ace the race competition, but he is avoiding practice and instead indulging in some other activity. Hence, attaining that goal is put off subconsciously through such resistance. Thus, resistance is not resilience.

In some way, they relate to each other in the sense that you may need to resist the urge to do something unhealthy to be resilient.

Let's consider a scenario:

You are offered a high-paying desirable job, but its location is hundreds of miles from where you live with your children. You have many reasons to take the job in terms of benefits and work-life balance, but there are also significant changes in your children's lives. They might lose friends, a familiar community, and a social circle for a new place where they have to make a new start.

In such scenarios, resilient kids will "look on the bright side" and see the new beginning as an adventure, as they will have new places and people to see. I know leaving friends and family behind will be sad, but resilient kids will quickly adapt to their new life, make new friends, experience new cultures, and continue to grow.

However, children accustomed to resistance may experience negative feelings of despair and unhappiness with change. Such children lack the adaptability and flexibility to adjust to change. They take enormous time to get familiar with and settle in a place. In changing environments, they often despair and have trouble coping with new situations in schools and society. They "get stuck" in the past without looking toward the future. Hence, they resist moving on.

Though it is not easy to cope with sudden and abrupt life changes, one has to try their best, as we want our children to adapt to new environments without any resistance. This can only happen if they are resilient enough to adapt and resist falling into despair.

Do you see the circle? Resistance and resilience are two superpowers that go together. Resilience and resistance bifurcate and combine into one. Our children must know where to adapt and when to resist.

Resilience Vs. Persistence

Like resistance and resilience, persistence is a high-value quality. It is similar to endurance and resilience, yet drawing the difference for clarity is necessary. Persistence, like resilience, is also a superpower. The Oxford Dictionary defines persistence as" continuing in an opinion or course of action despite difficulty or opposition." It is about standing tall and authentic for what one is, no matter what others say. Whereas resilience is staying authentic in one's power and facing predicaments to solve them.

Consider this inspiring scenario: Assume you have raised courageous, bold, and nonjudgmental children. A fresh student is enrolled in their school and is bullied by snobs. If your children stick to their principles, they will go against the mainstream and strive to stand up to bullying courageously. With an astute mix of persistence and resilience, anchored in their values, they will stand up to bullies and solve the bullying problem. For example, a resilient and persistent kid would organize a game or some collective activity, inviting both the bully and the new kid. This way, an activity involving cooperation or teamwork will make other kids get acquainted and possibly become friends. Hence, they discourage bullying and help channel the negative attitude into a positive activity.

Though it is a simple example, the spirit of the idea remains the same. Persist resiliently, despite opposition.

Jay Wren has explained it beautifully:

> "Persistence (that is, staying at a task until you achieve success) and resilience (that is, returning to a task to find new ways to achieve success) go hand in hand" ("Persistence and Resilience," 2021).

The difference comes in when there are other scenarios to consider. Persistence is more related to who is strong enough to "swim upstream" and who can survive the worst of the worst. Resilience, however, is not simply swimming through but, adapting, asking for help, and growing.

Resilience Vs. Perseverance

Perseverance is another term quite similar to persistence and can be confused with resilience; however, it is slightly different. Perseverance means" persistence in doing something despite difficulty or delay in achieving success ."It is the continued effort and energy one puts in to achieve a goal. According to Scher:

> Resilience is defined as "an ability to recover from or adjust easily to misfortune or change," and perseverance is defined as "the continued effort to do or achieve something despite difficulties, failure, or opposition" (Scher, 2013).

Let us consider a scenario where a child struggles with schoolwork. He faces multiple challenges: bullying, trouble making friends, and being poor in academics and sports. Eventually, he needs more motivation to study or improve, which leads to bad grades. In such a scenario, a resilient child will try to solve the issues of poor grades or bullying. He will seek help from his parents and teachers and access resources to plan out learning strategies and exam techniques to get better grades, no matter how many times he fails. In contrast, a persevering child would stay determined to keep going despite how tough the storm gets. He will try to sail alone, even without a silver lining. He will remain committed to giving his best. Their hard work is their superpower.

Both resilience and perseverance are essential qualities for the child mentioned above. Resilience helps the child adapt to the challenges, while perseverance enables them to continue their efforts toward their goal.

WHY DOES IT MATTER?

We all want our children to grow up strong, confident, and capable of navigating the ups and downs of life. Teaching our children resilience is like giving them a gift that will never expire or break—an inner strength that will help them overcome obstacles and thrive in a rapidly changing world.

By nurturing resilience in our children, we prepare them to face the inevitable challenges they will encounter along their journey. Some of the challenges that most (if not all) children face include:

- Bullying happens, no matter how many measures are implemented to counter it. Resilience empowers them to stand up for themselves, get the support they need, and develop strategies to cope with bullying. Self-esteem is essential when you're a kid, and bullying could even lead to deadly consequences if we do not teach our children to be resilient enough to work through it.
- Social interactions are complex for some children (not all), leading to isolation and/or loneliness. Resilient children can adapt, build social skills, and forge new connections even in unfamiliar situations. When you were in school, you would spend hours stressing over tests; Our kids do too. Resilience helps children develop problem-solving skills and maintain a growth mindset; we'll discuss the mindset more later on!

- Friends always fight, even the best of friends. In fact, the best of friends often fight the most! Resilient children can navigate through conflicts, negotiate differences, and mend relationships.

Signs of Resilient Kids

How do we recognize resilience in our kids? What does a resilient child look like? Let's look at a few scenarios where their strength and resilience might be visible.

- Picture this: Your child has been working hard on a school project for weeks through sleepless nights and early mornings. Despite their efforts, they receive a "C" and not an "A.". A resilient child would feel disappointed initially, just like anyone else would. Still, instead of giving up, they would see it as a learning experience. The feedback is taken as constructive, and they identify areas for improvement. They maintain their motivation, learn from their mistakes, and grow stronger.
- Now picture two best friends arguing. Instead of dwelling on the conflict, a resilient child would communicate effectively and handle the situation better by expressing their feelings assertively, listening to their friend's perspective, and working towards finding a resolution.

- Let's picture divorce: it's not something we want to think about if we're happily married, but it's a fact of daily life. A resilient child would absolutely be upset or sad, but they would look for that little "silver lining," even if it means two peaceful homes instead of one warzone. Resilient kids would not let the sadness of their parting family keep them down for long; they would stand right back up and take on a new journey, and they would accept the fact of life, which is that parents are separated for the better.

Resilient kids stand out in the way they handle setbacks, conflicts, and transitions. By providing them with support, encouragement, and opportunities for growth, we empower them to become resilient individuals who can face life's challenges head-on.

You might be wondering how one can build resilience in children during these trying times. That's what this book is all about. But first, let's cover some common challenges that kids (and we) face in building resilience. Nobody said it would be easy, but I hope that this first chapter has demonstrated why it's essential and why it would be worth it.

> Resilient kids are healthy kids; healthy kids are happy kids.

CHAPTER 2

COMMON CHALLENGES WITH BUILDING RESILIENCE

What gets in the way of building resilience?

This chapter aims to answer that question by listing common childhood occurrences and situations that could hinder a child's ability to cultivate resilience, yet how to bounce back from adverse experiences.

THE WORLD IS NOT A BED OF ROSES BUT FULL OF THORN-LIKE challenges. It does not matter what age, nation, or race we belong to; we will face many challenges throughout life. To ride the rough terrain of life, which is full of obstacles from cradle to grave, we must teach something essential to our children to survive successfully. For that to happen, we should be able to identify some of life's significant challenges and offer our help accordingly. If we can give our children a childhood that trains them to be resilient, that will make them resilient adults. As childhood is a crucial part of our lives, it determines and shapes the psychological development of our child's personality. If childhood experiences are healthy and one has coped with challenges in a healthy way, then chances are that one will grow up with a resilient nature and character. However, if childhood experiences are harmful, they can lead to severe damage and shortcomings in a child's personality.

CHILDHOOD STRESS AND TRAUMATIC EVENTS

Childhood can be a joyful repository of blissful moments in life, yet at the same time, it can also be a host of many challenging experiences. These childhood experiences mold us to who we are and immensely impact our adult lives. The kind of personality we are going to have, the kind of attitude we will exhibit, and how we will show up in intimate relationships- patterns of our childhood conditioning hugely impact all this. Hence, there can be things that are beyond ordinary that can leave a lasting impact on a child's life. We must understand the humungous impact that stress and trauma can have on the psychological and cognitive development of the child and his ability to foster resilience.

A traumatic event or toxic parenting can impact a child's emotional development and make it more difficult for him to develop social and interpersonal skills to deal with life's challenges.

Here are some childhood traumas that could have a negative effect:

- Children who experience social anxiety or have trouble with their self-esteem may find it harder to make friends and develop healthy relationships. These difficulties may disrupt their ability to build resilience. They may be more prone to avoid social situations, act shy, and shrink in a gathering, leading to limited opportunities for developing essential social skills.
- The loss of a family member or a loved one, such as a parent, grandparent, aunt/uncle, or even a friend, has an unimaginable impact on a child's emotional well-being. This loss can result in feelings of sadness, confusion, and even guilt. Coping with such trauma requires tremendous support and understanding from parents and/or caregivers to help children navigate their grief and build resilience.
- Health issues, be it physical or mental illness, personality disorders, and even addiction in parents or family members, can profoundly affect children. In such a case, they may lack the stability and support to develop resilience properly.

- Any childhood abuse will likely have a long-lasting impact on a child's well-being and resilience. Overcoming the trauma of abuse requires professional intervention and a safe and supportive environment. Building resilience in such cases involves healing, rebuilding trust, and helping children develop healthy coping mechanisms. In such a case, it may take time and a lot of patience.

- Separation from the person who has raised them so far, whether due to divorce, foster care, or other circumstances, can profoundly impact a child's sense of security and attachment. Losing a stable and nurturing relationship can cause emotional distress and disrupt their resilience-building journey. It is crucial to provide stability, consistent support, and open communication during these transitions to help children rebuild trust, adapt, and develop resilience.

Raising a child is no less than a feat in these tumultuous times. While we cannot control everything in life, there are some things that we can do to protect our children against the storms of life. We might be unable to stop the storm, but we can provide an umbrella at least. Hence, we ought neither to become overprotective nor too indifferent; instead, we have to support them through their journey and also support ourselves. Childhood traumas affect not only them but us as well. So, we not only have to tend to their needs, but we also have to 'co-manage' ourselves.

The most important thing to remember is to look out for the mental well-being of your child and the way you take care of their physical health. Sometimes, things can get out of control and, if not paid due attention, might lead to grave consequences. In such extraordinary situations, one has to take drastic measures to address the crisis or problem in their child's life. I have often observed that some parents don't admit immediately that their child may need help. While you may not want to bring your child to a psychiatrist, like me, right away, what you can do is help them see a psychologist, therapist, or counselor. Seeing a mental health professional might be the best place to start. From there on, if necessary, depending on the severity of the problem, the therapist might refer you to a specialist psychiatrist, like me, to provide additional care.

Childhood trauma cannot heal itself. It requires patience and a long-term healing process. Its handling or first diagnosis often begins with some form of therapy. As there are various kinds of treatments, it is up to you to decide what is best for your child.

In some cases, talk therapy, CBT, or other non-medicinal therapy might not help after a certain point. In such instances, medication can become essential. Also, I want you all to know that taking medicine for a mental health issue, whether for trauma or any other reason, is not something to be ashamed of. Like we take medication when we are physically ill, when mentally ill, we also need medicine that can make us feel healthy and lively. Though a stigma is attached to prescribing mental health medications to children, I want to set the record straight. If you or your child can have a fuller or more blissful life, and the only way to do so is through medication, then I urge you to trust your healthcare providers. It is not what the media wants us to believe!

CHILDHOOD INSTABILITY

> Instability includes disruptions to a child's life including frequent moves, changes in schools, unpredictable family dynamics, financial hardships, or any circumstances that bring about sudden and unexpected changes (Sandstrom & Huerta, 2013).

Instability refers to sudden disruptions and frequent unpredictable changes in life that can profoundly affect a child's ability to build resilience. Some children can become resilient after being exposed to instability if they have the necessary tools to navigate the situation. A child's mental and cognitive development can suffer without essential coping mechanisms and skills.

Unmanaged instability can be crippling for your child's development. Constant instability can lead to high levels of stress, anxiety, and uncertainty. The more upheavals, the more uncertainty, as both are related. Hence, an unstable childhood can lead to uncertainty and create issues of mistrust that can be shored up later in the child's life.

Constant instability means there is not enough time for your kid to make sense of his surroundings as everything is in flux. Hence, the child does not have enough time to adapt to new situations; being "thrown around from one place to another" can make one's head spin, making it difficult to find one's footing.

Many of you would be wondering that change is part of life, and sometimes it's for good. I understand it's part of life, but the rate at which things change must be observed carefully. Sometimes things cannot be helped, but when they can, we must try our best. There is no doubt that eventually, kids will adapt to rapid changes and get used to hopping around, but what kind of life would that be? How would such a life be when one can never call a city home or get a sense of belonging to a place? In such cases, kids unconsciously learn that nothing is permanent or certain and can never form lasting bonds with people around them. This can lead to serious social anxiety issues and hamper the development of other social skills crucial for practical life.

Unstable environment leads to uncertainty. And if the kid does not have the time to adapt and thrive, it causes a pause or delay in developing resilience. In such a scenario, the presence of a stable family member or caregiver is of high importance. When a child has an adult they can trust, look up to, and depend on during times of instability, their chances of healthy development immensely increase. Hence, even if the surrounding has changed, a stable caregiver in their life can serve as an anchor for them so that they can steer their path, even in times of crisis.

Despite how much I want to say that the presence of a stable caregiver can help a child's social development; unfortunately, too much reliance upon a parental figure can make a child dependent on them. This can hinder a child from forming good social relationships with his peers. Though one can come out clean through a crisis when a supportive adult is there, it is difficult for a child to adjust socially with his fellows when one is used to adult company.

A stable parent figure serves as a nest, a grounding anchor for the ship of a child's life. It provides a secure foundation for the child to explore and take risks. The strong foundation thus established provides the child with a reassuring presence, a dependable support system, and a guide in adversity, allowing him to foster trust and confidence in his abilities to thrive in the face of challenges.

A stable childhood leads to a secure attachment style and builds emotional resilience. Especially the kid who has a stable and supportive parental figure is more likely to feel comfortable expressing his emotions, seeking help, and taking the initiative in overcoming challenges. If there is too much change and flux in your family life, and there is always too much going on, then becoming a supportive anchor for your child would be a step in the right direction.

We, as parents, should try to create a stable and safe home environment. This means consistent routines, open communication, and expressing feelings freely. We must be a reliable source of support and comfort that offers guidance and reassurance during difficult times. They always say that charity begins at home, and it applies here as well, albeit in a non-traditional context.

This means that you must look out for your family before you can turn your attention to anything else. One has to put one's house in order before tending to society's matters. Our priority as family leaders should be cultivating a safe, stable, and non-judgmental environment in our homes, where communication and expressing feelings are encouraged rather than snubbed. Once we have done that, we can figure out ways of dealing with any problem.

If instability persists in a child's life, consider seeking additional support through therapists, counselors, or community resources. These professionals can provide tools and strategies to help both children and parents navigate the challenges associated with instability and build resilience. We're here because we want to help each other. Also, by sharing my findings and experiences, I am assisting other parents like myself. I'd like you to do the same: share your resources with others in need.

Unlike yesteryears, when women were dubbed as hysterical for showing any signs of mental illness and issues of children's psyche were usually ignored, thankfully, today, we have ample studies and research to help us treat problems related to child development.

"Parenting and the home environment act as a buffer between instability and the child. When they are positive and supportive, parents can protect the child from the effects of instability; however, instability can potentially weaken the quality of parenting and the home environment, thus negatively influencing the child" (Sandstrom & Huerta, 2013).

Eventually, resilience is not just about kids. It is about us too. Not only do we have to make sure our kids are resilient, but we, as parents, should also become resilient. Family as a unit has to be resilient; this can only happen if each member is resilient. A chain is as strong as its smallest rung. However, having a strong and resilient parent figure is needed for positive outcomes, but more is required if only one person is carrying all the weight. Just like the school of fish in the popular children's movie "Finding Nemo," they swam together down to the bottom of the ocean to break the net from the fishing boat that had captured them. One fish could not have done it, but together, they did. The moral of the story is: we are strong when we are united. As in togetherness lies strength.

"During difficult life circumstances, families implement coping strategies, such as turning to their support networks and community resources, to effectively manage the stress. Effective coping, or family resiliency, leads to adaptation that can restore balance to the family's functioning. The overarching view is that, when parents face extremely stressful life situations and are unable to effectively cope, their ability to provide the necessary resources and support for their children is constrained. Their children then experience a great deal of unbuffered stress—potentially toxic stress, in the most extreme cases—and have more difficulties reaching their full potential, academically and socially" (Sandstrom & Huerta, 2013).

CHILDHOOD ADVERSITY

It is not uncommon for children to encounter adversity throughout their lives, even into adulthood. Childhood adversity refers to experiences that pose significant challenges or hardships to a child's well-being and development. Normal adversity in a limited quantity isn't necessarily a bad thing. But severe adversity can have effects such as these:

- emotional and psychological consequences
- interference with cognitive processes including attention, memory, and problem-solving skills

- behavioral challenges and changes
- inability to form and maintain healthy relationships, leading to difficulties in trust, attachment, and social interactions.

Adversity can specifically affect resilience development in the following ways:

- Adversity often disrupts the presence of protective factors, such as a stable and nurturing caregiver, supportive relationships, and access to resources. These factors play a crucial role in fostering resilience.
- Children facing significant adversity may struggle to develop and effectively use coping strategies.
- Adversity may lead to negative self-perception and lowered self-esteem.
- The impact of childhood adversity can lead to developmental delays, affecting crucial milestones and skills necessary for the development of resilience.

The Relationship Between Resilience and Adversity

It's important to recognize the potential for resilience to emerge from adversity.

The relationship between resilience and adversity is as follows:

- Identifying *protective factors* such as supportive relationships and access to resources can enhance resilience.
- Teaching children healthy *coping skills* and fostering a growth mindset can empower them to navigate adversity and further develop resilience.
- Encouraging the formation of *social support*—or supportive relationships—can provide children with additional sources of resilience and guidance.
- *Trauma-informed approaches* play a key role. Recognizing the potential impact of trauma resulting from childhood adversity can help create a safe and supportive environment for children to heal and build resilience.

UNCOVER BULLYING

We all know what bullying is and have experienced or observed it many times in our lives. It is an obstruction that hinders the development of resilience in kids. Let us dive a little deeper into the bullying phenomenon so we can better understand it and eventually find a solution.

Bullying is a serious problem that is often overlooked in our schools, educational institutions, social settings, and even the workplace. Parents and authority figures usually ignore it or dismiss it as child play. However, these small micro-aggressions and mean attitudes can cause real damage to kids' well-being. In these tech-driven, fast times, bullying is worse than ever. It is a social malady that has infested our schools. It can crush spirits, belittle self-esteem, and psychologically affect a child's mental health. At worst, it can lead to suicide and self-loathing. Though discussing suicide is difficult, we should not be afraid to do so when our child's fate is at stake.

Now think of it this way: if you have a very open and friendly relationship with your kid, you might think you know all about them. However, there will still be things the child might hide from you. He might be hesitant or embarrassed to share the experience that he went through. And it is possible because bullies usually have a very fearful psychological control over your child. They can psychologically mess with people's heads and sometimes get under the skin. Some of you might think their child is different and their relationship is excellent. Yet there is a sheer possibility that the child may be scared or embarrassed to share it. As parents, we know this can lead to more severe issues than bullying alone.

Bullying is not simply playing macho or big-man; rather, bullying is much more than we traditionally think of. Cases as serious as physical harm, abuse, or even sexual abuse reported in schools worldwide can be linked to extreme bullying. I cannot stress enough how important it is for parents to foster and nurture an open, trustworthy relationship with their kids starting at a young age. Teach them there are no secrets, and sharing some embarrassing details won't leave them in hot water. Reassure them, gain their confidence, and be their confidante!

Now, here is the glitch: Your child might want to tackle the issue independently, which is admirable. However, they should feel comfortable asking for help when they need it. They should understand that saying, "Hey Mom/dad, I need help, is okay."Seeking help does not mean they're not resilient or "strong." I believe that asking for help and learning is indeed the real meaning of being "strong."

If you suspect your child may be a victim of bullying, then follow your instincts, and investigate the situation. Sit them down and talk to them, ask teachers to observe their behavior, and do something. Just don't play it off as "nothing."

Indicators of Possible Bullying

- bruises, cuts, swelling, other physical signs
- excessive sleepiness or insomnia
- eating more or less than usual
- unwillingness to go to school
- withdrawing into themselves
- acting out, rebelling, or other forms of defying authority
- skipping classes or not performing as well as they used to in school

All these obstacles and challenges presented henceforth can be overcome with a strong mindset. A resilient mindset with a 'never give up' attitude is the perfect panacea for facing these challenges. But what exactly is a growth mindset? It's a territory we will mark in the next chapter.

3

RESILIENCE AND THE GROWTH MINDSET

It is hard to fail but it is worse never to have tried to succeed.

—THEODORE ROOSEVELT

In this chapter, we will go through what the growth mindset is and how it is related to resilience. As it is said, we cannot always choose what happens in the external environment, but what we can do is respond to it. We are our thoughts. Our mind is the greatest tool; if we can think big, we can become a big success, and if we think small, we remain small. Mindset, the way we think, makes all the difference in attaining goals or bringing great detriment.

WHAT IS A GROWTH MINDSET?

A growth mindset is the belief that skills, intelligence, and talent can be improved through dedication, hard work, zest, and willingness to learn. A mindset is a frame of mind that can serve as a robust tool for our kids to cultivate resilience.

The power of the growth mindset is almost inexplicable. It can be better explained by contrasting it with what it is not: a fixed mindset. A fixed mindset refers to the belief that we are born with certain innate qualities and talents that make us who we are and that we cannot be anything else. Individuals with a fixed mindset see challenges and problems in life as threats to their self-worth, and they think of failures as evidence of their limitations, as they do not possess a certain kind of skill or talent. However, on the other hand, a growth mindset sees life's challenges as opportunities for growth and honing new skills. Individuals with such a mindset know that new experiences can teach new skills, and resilience can be nurtured, improving their lives and chances of success. A growth mindset encourages one to go a long way if one puts in the hard work, remains consistent, learns from failure, and shows perseverance.

There are many advantages to encouraging a growth mentality in our children—maybe too many to enumerate in one book, much less one chapter. It promotes adaptability, resilience, and a passion for learning. Because they understand that their hard work and dedication will result in advancement and personal development, our youngsters become more driven, tenacious, and willing to take on challenges to pursue their goals.

Some practical strategies to help cultivate a growth mindset:

- Focus on acknowledging the effort and hard work your child puts into their activities, projects, or anything. Rather than praising their achievements, reinforce the belief that progress comes from dedication and resilience.
- Create an environment that values exploration and embraces new experiences. Encourage your child to take on challenges and view mistakes as opportunities to learn and grow.
- Demonstrate a growth mindset in your actions and reactions. Share your struggles and setbacks and how you overcame them. Keeping it age-appropriate, of course.
- Offer specific and constructive feedback that focuses on areas of improvement rather than harsh criticism. Encourage your child to see feedback as a valuable tool for growth and development. Kids need to know that feedback, especially the constructive kind, is valuable and helpful in our journey to growth.

Common Misconceptions Regarding Growth Mindsets

There are some famous misconceptions regarding a growth mindset. Let's break them down one by one.

> 1. Having a growth mindset means believing you can do anything.

A growth mindset does not imply that you can do anything without limitations. It does not suggest that individuals can master every skill effortlessly. On the contrary, it suggests that attaining something requires hard work, and failure is part of the journey. Failures are nothing but rungs of the success ladder.

> 2. A growth mindset eliminates the need for natural talent or abilities.

That's not factual at all. Actually, a growth mindset acknowledges that people are different. It does not nullify natural abilities but emphasizes that hard work is crucial in nurturing, refining, and developing those talents. A growth mindset encourages individuals to embrace their strengths while simultaneously seeking growth and improvement.

> **3.** A growth mindset means always being positive and avoiding negative emotions.

Some may feel that having a growth mindset is always remaining positive, attempting to be joyful regardless of circumstances, and avoiding negative emotions. Such an exaggerated positivity is "toxic" whereas, in reality, a growth mindset recognizes every single negative emotion and, rather than running from it, tends to it until it becomes a lesson for learning.

Let's dig a little deep into the difference between a growth mindset versus a fixed mindset through the help of some hypothetical examples.

SCENARIO	FIXED MINDSET	GROWTH MINDSET
A talent competition is hosted at school, and many children take part. Like with many other school activities, there is a level of what is supposed to be healthy competition. Billy has his heart set on winning first prize, but he comes in third.	Billy believes that he failed because he's just not that good at what he thought was his talent and moves on to something else.	Billy accepts his third prize award with a smile because he still placed, and he is determined to work harder to get even better, but he also understands that it isn't all about winning. He got to share his passion with the crowd.

Mary bakes cupcakes for school. It's her first time doing so. She's excited to present them to her friends in class. It's her birthday, and she wants to share her happiness with her classmates. Unfortunately, the first few cringe after their first bites, and they spit the cupcake out.	Mary feels defeated. She decides to never try baking again and opts to ask her parents to purchase cupcakes from the store instead.	Mary is upset, but she giggles at the faces her classmates make, asking them what it tastes like. She determines that she has added too much salt. She invites her friends over to her house to help her bake new cupcakes over the weekend, making sure they carefully measure all the ingredients.
There is a massive event being held in town. The person with the biggest pumpkin wins a grand prize. The Everson's have been growing pumpkins all their lives, but they're hesitant to take part because of all the other pumpkin farmers around who have a wonderful crop.	They decide not to take part in order to avoid humiliation or disappointment.	They enter the competition despite the chance that they may not win because it will still be a lot of fun, and they can learn tips from other people who also grow pumpkins.
Katherine watched the graceful finger strokes of Richard Clayderman on television all her life while dreaming of being a famous pianist. Nobody else in her family plays any musical instruments, and though she has tried before, she hasn't been able to really learn much.	Katherine accepts that the "musical gene" is just not in her family and that there is nothing she can do about it. She spends her days longing for what she believes she can never have.	Katherine is determined to learn—come hell or high water. Even if it takes years, this is her dream, and she will fight for it. After two years of hard work, Katherine performs at her local church.

Cody and Sebastian have been best friends since they were children. They both have a great love for athletic sports. The big race comes up, and Cody wins the race. Of course, he is thrilled. However, Sebastian is gutted.	Sebastian sees Cody's success as a threat, and the friendship begins to deteriorate.	Sebastian cheers for Cody and feels inspired to work hard to share a victory one day. Cody and Sebastian train together, and Sebastian wins the next race. They cheer for each other's successes.
Claire loves painting. Upon graduation, she is accepted into art school. Back home, people adored her art, and she was praised daily. However, this is a big city, and everyone is an artist. Claire receives criticism for her work for the very first time.	Claire gets defensive, and angry. She feels hurt and insists that whoever is in charge must not like her. Her time at the school is miserable, and her passion begins to crumble.	Claire is fascinated by the views of other artists, and soaks in every bit of advice that she can. The criticism is constructive, and she learns a great deal over the next few years, furthering her passion and skill.
Christian fails math tests over and over again. His family cannot help him because nobody is really good at math.	Christian feels as though his intelligence is below that of his peers, and retrieves into himself. He believes that his intelligence is what it is, and he'll just never be a star performer with any of his grades.	Christian is determined to do better, he knows his intelligence, regardless of what that entails, is determined on how hard he works, and what he shapes it into.

I'd also like to share a personal story that recently happened to my very own daughter. She has a very outstanding musical talent and sings beautifully. Her music teacher has always adored her. Her church pastor suggested that she sign up for Teen Talent, representing the church that she attends on Wednesdays.

Unfortunately, she didn't have enough time to prepare because she was in the middle of her exams. She still took part, though, feeling a sense of obligation. She didn't place at all and knew she didn't do well. I thought my girl would be devastated. Instead, her reaction astounded me. She smiled and said that she was alright with not ranking.

You might be wondering about what had gone in her head. Her reasoning? Because she knew that it was a big competition and included hundreds of talents from all over Florida. Although she is used to being one of the best at school, she recognized that she is compared with a much smaller group of kids at her medium-sized private school. Her perception of the entire scenario was heart-warming: She realized that when the competition is much bigger, and she is competing with the best of the best, she may not be the best, but it does not mean she is a failure. She continues to love her voice and knows she is talented. In addition, she recognizes the talents of others and praises them instead of wallowing in despair.

Another similar instance involving my daughter was when her group of friends auditioned for the cheerleading squad, and many of her friends got on the team, but she didn't. This upset her, and rightfully so. It was something she strongly desired but couldn't get. It's normal for children to feel disappointed when they work for something and it doesn't go well. However, even though she felt upset, she said she felt proud of herself for trying. She knew that she wasn't really ready yet; she had only just started practicing. The lesson learned is that you don't always get what you want the very first time. Many of the other team members had been practicing cheerleading for years. She knew that she would have had a better chance if she had worked harder and longer.

As a mother, I was proud of her in both instances. She recognized that she was talented but still needed to work hard. She learned that it's okay to not be the best, especially when thrown into a much bigger pond. She also learned that if she doesn't bring her "A" game, she might not reach that goal, which means that next time, she'll know that she needs to put more work in.

HOW A GROWTH MINDSET HELPS BUILD RESILIENCE

A growth mindset and resilience share a reciprocal relationship—each contributing to the development and enhancement of the other.

A growth mindset fosters resilience. When children possess a growth mindset, they are more likely to embrace challenges, view setbacks as learning opportunities, and persist in the face of obstacles.

Resilience nurtures a growth mindset. Through experiences of resilience, children learn that setbacks are not insurmountable barriers but rather stepping stones for growth. This mindset of resilience then fuels their belief in their capacity to learn, improve, and develop a growth mindset.

There is an intersection between growth mindset and resilience. While a growth mindset and resilience are intertwined, it is important to note that they are not synonymous. While a child with a growth mindset may be more likely to develop resilience and vice versa, they are distinct concepts.

Growth mindset lays the foundation for resilience. A child with a growth mindset is more likely to approach challenges with resilience and navigate setbacks with a determination to overcome them.

Resilience is a reflection of a growth mindset. When a child is resilient, it does not necessarily guarantee the presence of a growth mindset. Resilience can stem from various factors such as supportive relationships, coping strategies, and self-belief—regardless of their perspective about intelligence or abilities.

A growth mindset and resilience are intimately intertwined, each reinforcing and supporting the other. While a growth mindset can contribute to the development of resilience, resilience itself is not solely indicative of a growth mindset.

HOW TO FOSTER A GROWTH MINDSET IN CHILDREN

> "Risky play in early childhood can help develop a child's self-confidence, resilience, executive functioning abilities, and even risk-management skills. And Brussoni's work in injury prevention research shows that engaging in risky play can actually reduce the risk of injury, too" (Toole, n.d.).

To promote a growth mindset, it's important to encourage our kids to take healthy risks within reason. Read that again: within reason. No need for adrenaline hunters to get all riled up; that's not what we're talking about here.

Here's What You Can Do

Start by explaining the concept of healthy risk-taking to your children. Let them know that it involves trying new things, exploring their interests, and stepping outside their comfort zones. Emphasize the importance of assessing risks to ensure their safety, though. We don't want kids trying to fly off the roof.

Explain the Difference Between Healthy and Reckless Risks

Flying off the roof: Yes, that would be a reckless risk. Help your children understand the difference between healthy risks and reckless risks. Encourage them to evaluate potential consequences and make informed decisions. Set clear boundaries and empower your children to make responsible choices.

Explain to them how engaging in new experiences fosters self-confidence, resilience, and the development of essential skills. Your kids might be kids, but they're still people. Talk to them. Tell them what happens when you take a healthy risk such as risking your reputation by taking part in a new game versus what happens when you stick your finger in a lion's cage. Be honest with them while considering age-appropriateness.

Failures

Children need to understand that failure is not something to fear but an essential part of the learning journey.

Remember the following:

- Normalize failure.
- Encourage a growth mindset.
- Praise effort and encourage mindful risk-taking.
- Applaud their acts of courageous initiative and standing up for what is right.
- Celebrate them trying their best.

It's difficult to remember to include these tips in our lives. The world we live in is broken; the winners are praised, and the failures are treated poorly. Schools typically test children for good grades, not for the work they've put in. The child who worked the hardest often doesn't get a thing. That's where we come in. If the world won't give them the praise and warmth they deserve, we will.

Balancing Praise

While it is important to acknowledge and celebrate your child's achievements, it is equally crucial to strike a balance. Avoid excessive and insincere praise that may create a false sense of accomplishment. Instead, focus on specific aspects of their effort, progress, or the lessons they have learned. This is something that I firmly believe in, but some may not understand the meaning of striking a balance right off the bat. Therefore, we'll use a few anecdotes to elaborate on the topic.

First Anecdote

Six-year-old Marli was very pleased with herself for drawing a full face, complete with a nose, ears, eyes, a mouth, and everything in between. Her parents praised her, and that was good. It was a true achievement. The next day, she brought another picture to them, and it was very similar to the first. Once again, they loudly praised her work. This went on for days. Eventually, Marli stopped showing them her pictures because she could feel that they were being insincere. Children are smarter than we think, and even when she presented them with pictures of cats and dogs that were not really up to scratch, they praised her. This led to her doubting herself because if they always praise her, is she really any good at anything?

This may sound like complex emotions for a six-year-old, but believe me—they pick up on it. Children of any age likely will pick up on insincere praises eventually, and it will become discouraging—even damaging to their self-esteem in the long run.

Second Anecdote

A personal friend of mine—let's call her Jenna—had a teenage son who longed to be on the school's football team. At the time, I absolutely encouraged her to support him. That's what most parents would do, right? Johnny didn't make the team the last time he tried out, and as expected, he was encouraged to work hard this time in order to achieve his goal.

He worked around the clock, but unfortunately, he did not make the team again. Instead of praising him for working hard to achieve a goal and for doing his best, Jenna lashed out at the coach for picking on her son. She called him a "star performer" and continued to praise him for his skills.

This is an example of Momma Bear going a little too far. Sometimes, our children do need to accept that something may just not be for them, but they can still be celebrated for hard work and encouraged to try something else. In such a case, it's important to remain enthusiastic. Even if a child is absolutely gutted, try to keep spirits high.

A better response would have been as follows: "Well, you did great. You worked really hard, and I'm proud of you. Your school has many other sports! Why don't you try hockey next? I hear they travel to amazing places for games."

Benefits of Learning to Navigate Failure

- Children who learn to navigate failure develop stronger problem-solving abilities. They become more adaptable, creative, and skilled at finding alternative approaches to overcoming challenges.
- Children who understand that failure is a stepping stone are more likely to flourish in the face of difficulties, leading to greater achievement in the long run.
- Children who embrace failure cultivate a growth mindset—our goal on the path to building resilience.

GROWTH MINDSET ACTIVITIES

When it comes to teaching children valuable life skills including resilience and growth mindset, hands-on activities and play are incredibly effective.

ACTIVITIES FOR KIDS

PUZZLE POWER

Engage your child in puzzles and brain teasers that challenge their problem-solving abilities. Encourage them to persevere, take different approaches, and celebrate small victories along the way.

GROWTH MINDSET JOURNAL

Introduce a growth mindset journal where your child can write or draw about their experiences, challenges, and what they've learned ("Growth Mindset," n.d.). Encourage them to reflect on their progress, setbacks, and how they can approach similar situations differently in the future.

STORYTIME EXPLORATION

Choose books that highlight characters who face challenges and overcome obstacles through perseverance and a growth mindset. After reading, discuss the story together, focusing on the characters' mindsets and the lessons learned.

SCAVENGER HUNT OF LEARNING

Organize a scavenger hunt where your child discovers different learning opportunities in their surroundings. Hide clues that lead them to books, art supplies, or educational activities. Encourage them to embrace the challenge, problem-solve, and enjoy the process of discovery.

COOKING ADVENTURES

Involve your child in the kitchen by letting them participate in age-appropriate cooking tasks. Encourage them to try new recipes, experiment with flavors, and learn from any culinary mishaps.

NATURE'S CLASSROOM

Take your child on nature walks or outdoor adventures, encouraging them to observe, ask questions, and discover the wonders of the natural world. Discuss the growth and changes they observe, relating them to personal growth and the importance of embracing challenges.

REFLECTION TIME

Set aside regular reflection time with your child where you discuss their experiences, setbacks, and achievements. Ask open-ended questions that encourage them to think critically and explore different perspectives. This practice helps them develop self-awareness and a growth mindset.

ACTIVITIES GEARED TOWARDS OLDER KIDS

Reflection time is something that older children can absolutely take part in, and so is Nature's Classroom. However, some older kids may be a little bored by the other activities, so let's look at what they can do instead.

POSTERS

This is something that I would recommend doing together. It's simply using posters to write down future goals and why they are important. Place them all over the house. This encourages your teen to work on their goals and reminds them why the goals are important.

BOOKMARKS AND MANTRAS

The older children get, the harder they need to read. Based on my research and experience, having bookmarks with encouraging mantras or quotes may help. A mantra is a simple phrase that can be repeated. To encourage your teen to push through the chapter, place bookmarks throughout their books. They can do this themselves, but it's all the more encouraging if they're pleasantly surprised by a bookmark placed there by a parent or caregiver. Mantras can be as simple as, "I can do this." Write it on a bookmark or simply encourage them to say it to themselves daily.

DISCOURAGE NEGATIVE SELF-TALK

You'll often hear teenagers repeat negativities about themselves. Discourage this, and have them repeat positive thinking instead (Tripple, 2021). When negativity consumes the mindset, it's nearly impossible to foster any kind of growth-mindset. When they say, "I hate school," encourage them to instead say, "I am grateful to be able to receive the education that many are not as fortunate to receive."

Yes, most teenagers will likely sigh when you ask them to say this instead. But it's just like a mantra; if said enough times, they will likely begin to believe it.

WINNER'S MINDSET

A winner's mindset is a form of growth-mindset. Encourage your teen to use visualization when they think about an upcoming challenge. Help them visualize the best possible scenario, but also to visualize the activity in general: the fun it will be to spend time with friends on the field and how exciting the competition will be. This encourages them to push harder in order to achieve that positive outcome, but it also reminds them that winning is not the most important thing. A former teen icon, Miley Cyrus, once said in her song "The Climb" that what matters most in life's situations is the climb itself. Cheesy, yet relatable for teens: Consider using it as an example of this concept.

In the next chapter, we will look at further practical strategies for helping kids cultivate resilience.

CHAPTER 4

BUILDING RESILIENCE IN KIDS

> Never has resilience—be it physical, mental, emotional or financial—been more important to our society than in the past year and a half, and never have I been so determined to pass it on to my son. He may not climb mountains, but life will always have a disaster, disappointment, or pandemic to throw his way. If he can't roll with the punches, his life will be very, very hard.
>
> **—ERIK VANCE**

UP UNTIL NOW, WE HAVE EXPLORED THE CHALLENGES AND hurdles that lie in the path of becoming resilient. We have seen how one may come across myriads of situations and predicaments that will test the strength of spirits in one's lifetime. In this chapter, we will figure out how to overcome those challenges; dodge those obstacles, and stand tall in our power when the whole world tries to bring us down. We will discuss some practical ways to grow resilience in children, the function of games in creating resilience, and the invaluable role that a supportive caregiver can play in fostering supportive relationships in this respect.

Are you ready for the next adventure?

ADDRESSING THE CHALLENGES

We have discussed various challenges one can encounter throughout different stages of life. It is often said that childhood is like a breeze in comparison to the storms of adulthood. But this is not the case for every child. Hence, as parents, seeing our children suffer would be the last thing we want. Therefore, no matter the situation, we need practical tips and strategies to help our kids. It is far worse to witness our child suffer and not be able to help him.

Let's look at a few of the challenges we've previously discussed.

- childhood stress and trauma
- childhood instability
- childhood adversity
- bullying

We've discussed these quite a bit; however, I would like to touch on them again with a few real-life stories from people I've met as a mother and psychiatrist.

For privacy, all names were changed to fictional names.

Childhood Stress and Trauma

Amanda was in her early thirties when we met by chance. Her story has stayed with me for many years. It was a traumatic story; trauma can be like a vicious cycle that keeps you in a loop. This was the nature of her story. She was raised by strict and controlling parents who beat her mercilessly. In truth, I don't even want to go into the details because it's too distressing.

She was plagued by trauma all her life. She was raised in such a way a part of her felt like "this is just how it is." Even though she had learned, with age, that it wasn't right, the subconscious imprinting remained. Thus, her first marriage was to an abusive man. Like many people subjected to trauma and went untreated, she simply tolerated the abuse like her childhood trauma bonded to an abusive partner.

Out of her abusive marriage, two children were born. Her husband dominated and controlled their life, in addition to hers. It wasn't until she watched him lash out at her youngest, grabbing his arm and tossing him onto a couch, that it finally hit her. At this moment, she realized that her children would grow up the way she did if she didn't make a change.

Her love for her kids helped her escape the abusive marriage, and she sought to refuge from a family friend. She broke the trauma bond and did away with the vicious cycle of abuse. Today, her eldest son is a college student, and her youngest is in high school. She has a job and a new life. She did marry again, and the second time, she was much more selective of the man she married.

The first right thing she did was to get out of there, and the second right thing she did was seek the professional help she needed. By getting the help she needed, she could better care for her children, and their resilience mirrored her own.

Unlike many others, this story has a happy ending. They became stronger on the other side, and Amanda bounced back harder than anyone I've met.

The practical strategies applied in the story above are simple to identify: she recognized and dealt with the problem.

It's not as easy as I make it sound here. Anyone who is or has been in a similar situation can attest to that. However, it is possible. Reaching out for help is your best strategy. It's alright to admit that you need help to get where you want or need to be. You'll be able to conquer it yourself in due time.

Amanda broke the toxic cycle and unlearned the unhealthy patterns she was conditioned to; The time is now to break any traumatic cycles that may have been plaguing your family.

Childhood Instability

I'll use Amanda as inspiration once again because, as you can imagine, there was quite a bit of instability in her life and the lives of her children.

Once Amanda began trying to get on her own feet, there were late nights of work, lots of moving around, and a lot of eating cereal for dinner. The constant changes in her sons' lives made it difficult for them to adapt. However, Amanda was determined to mend their lives, and thus she focused on research of her own regarding what she could do to help them be resilient in the face of constant change, helping them adapt.

Now they have a stable home. But just like Rome, that home was not built in a day.

The best thing you can do is research and constant learning. There are ways in which children can be helped in the face of instability, and with the aforementioned story, one thing was always a constant: They had their mother wherever they went. She loved, supported, and protected them fiercely, providing them with the needed stability.

Childhood Adversity

Adversity is a normal part of life. I remember a young girl I knew: I'll call her Sandy. She had a stable home and seemed to me to be just like any other teenager until I learned that the adversity she faced at school was traumatic.

Unfortunately, in the face of such adversity, she took her own life. Just like with bullying, it can often end badly. That's why we need to foster resilience in our children. Throughout my years of life, countless suicides due to adversity and bullying have been in the news—some even right under my radar. As a parent, I couldn't even begin to imagine the anguish and grief of losing a child due to such a thing.

Practically, we need to not only help children face these struggles with resilience, but we must also cultivate a caring and empathetic personality within them to ensure that our own do not become bullies.

We must provide them with a support system, and they must be aware of our presence. Even if they feel like nobody else, they need to know that they have us.

PRACTICAL STRATEGIES FOR CULTIVATING RESILIENCE IN CHILDREN

By listing some strategies and scenarios to illustrate them, let's see how we can further help young ones face life like the champions they are.

- Empower your child with problem-solving techniques. Encourage them to identify challenges, brainstorm possible solutions, and evaluate their effectiveness. This equips them with the tools to navigate obstacles independently.

Let's say that your child is struggling with a school project. Instead of solving it for them, you can guide them through breaking down the task into smaller, more manageable sections to find solutions.

- Help your child understand and manage their emotions effectively. Teach them to identify and express their feelings in a healthy way. This enables them to navigate challenges with emotional resilience.

    Let's say that your child is frustrated after a disappointing game. Instead of suppressing their emotions, you can guide them to identify their feelings and encourage them to express their disappointment constructively.

- Help your child to be just as compassionate towards themselves as they are to others by encouraging kindness, self-care, and self-understanding. Teach them to embrace their imperfections and practice self-acceptance.

    Let's say your child is upset after making a mistake. You can remind them that no one is perfect and everyone makes mistakes. A single mistake does not define them, and one learns through mistakes.

- Teach your children the importance of self-care from a young age—for their mental, physical, and emotional well-being. Encourage them to engage in activities they like, to get enough sleep, and to eat healthy foods.

Let's say your child is feeling overwhelmed with schoolwork. Suggest that taking a break and engaging in a relaxing activity is a good way to unwind the mind and prepare for the next study session.

- Be sure that your house is an inclusive and accepting environment where your children feel that they belong and not that they are outsiders.

Let's say your child is interested in a particular hobby or subject. You can support their passion by helping them find other like-minded people to share their interests and inviting them to your home!

- Encourage your child to think more "glass half full" rather than "glass half empty." Let them focus on the positives of situations, being grateful, and facing challenges positively.

Let's say that your child faces a setback in a sports competition. Encourage them not to dwell on the loss but to once again reflect on the experience, find positive aspects, and figure out what they can learn from it.

When your child feels discouraged about a difficult task, remind them of other achievements that they've reached. Highlight their progress thus far and encourage them to approach challenges with a positive mindset by celebrating small victories along the way.

ACTIVE INVOLVEMENT: PLAY AND EXPLORATION

While many factors contribute to resilience, play and exploration are powerful tools at our disposal. Do you remember how you used to pretend play when you were younger? Perhaps you created your magical world or pretended to be an archeologist or a doctor. That is a healthy part of growing up.

Physical Benefits

Play and exploration have many physical benefits that contribute to resilience in children. Physical activities help children develop strength, coordination, and gross motor skills. Pushing their physical boundaries will allow them to assess risks, overcome obstacles, and build physical resilience. Physical play is also healthy for their bodies since it promotes more movement. As they say, healthy body, healthy mind!

Emotional Benefits

Play and exploration encourage resilience in the face of emotional challenges ("The Brain Architects," n.d.). Children encounter situations that evoke many different emotions during their play. The playground becomes a training ground for life as they learn to regulate their emotions, manage stress, and cope with disappointments. This emotional resilience equips them with the skills to navigate relationships and cope with the ups and downs of life.

Psychological Benefits

Play allows children to engage their imagination and think critically. This encourages problem-solving and the art of making executive decisions. It's a great way to boost their self-confidence (NDFAuthors, 2023).

Allow children to engage in playtime where they can follow their interests and explore their creativity without predetermined outcomes or rules. While games such as Monopoly and musical chairs are fun, they're predictable. Let them spend more time in nature and get curious about the mysteries of nature. Your backyard is nature too, you know. A backyard can quickly become an enchanted forest for exploration!

Play and exploration are vital components in cultivating resilience in children. By recognizing play's physical, emotional, and psychological benefits and incorporating strategies to promote it in our children's lives, we empower them to develop resilience, adaptability, and confidence.

> Imagination is the key to a golden childhood.

RELATIONSHIPS: THE IMPORTANCE OF POSITIVE CONNECTIONS

The connection between positive relationships and a child's ability to cultivate resilience is a very important aspect of their lives as well ("Relationships and Child Development," 2023). We need to try to understand and encourage these relationships so that we can empower our children to develop the necessary skills to thrive both now and later in life.

Positive relationships nurture resilience in children. Besides parents, a child's support system may include siblings, teachers, friends, and more. These relationships can provide emotional support, guidance, and a sense of belonging, creating a safe and nurturing environment for children to develop resilience.

Children thrive when they have a good support system in place. We as their parents or caregivers are typically their most important and immediate support systems. However, the support system extends beyond just us, encompassing other people who positively contribute to their development as well.

Positive relationships also offer opportunities for kids to see healthy behaviors firsthand. When children witness positive interactions and effective communication, they learn these things for themselves more easily.

Supportive people provide encouragement and help our kids develop a growth mindset. Children who have positive relationships in their lives learn to persevere, adapt, and view failures as opportunities for growth.

Social connection is also important for building resilience. The support and social connection provided by these relationships function as protective factors against stress and adversity.

Providing opportunities for social connections is also important. We can support our kids when they take part in activities where they can form positive friendships and build meaningful connections. It's not always easy because we may not always be very supportive of their activities of choice. For example, many parents are not too happy about their kids joining the football team. Let's face it: It can be pretty dangerous. In such a case, we can research all safety measures and still support them to the best of our abilities. A team such as a football team often becomes like a little family, and they can form lifelong friendships.

The point is positive relationships are important. We do need to ensure that they are indeed positive, however. Be sure to pay close attention to their friends, what they talk about, and how they behave.

> Positive relationships = positive influences.

Authoritative Parenting

> "Children of authoritative parents are allowed to fail and learn from their mistakes. They build resilience, which is the ability to overcome and bounce back from life's challenges and traumas. These experiences also increase self-esteem, problem-solving skills, pride in accomplishments, and confidence" (Perry, 2022).

Of all the parenting styles out there, the best one by far is the authoritative parenting style. As explained in the quote above, it's still being firm, yet being kind and loving as well. It involves supporting your kids but having realistic expectations of them.

This means striking a fine balance between indifference and being too controlling. This refers to the fact of being present and friendly yet authoritative enough to maintain boundaries.

Think about the kind of a parent you are, and what kind of parent you want to become. My advice is to strive for an authoritative parenting style as a standard, and then compare how far and close you are to this parenting style. Your positive relationship with your child is just as important as their positive relationships with other people, where latter is dependent on the former.

Psychological resilience has a lot to do with your background. If you ensure that your kid's childhood is peaceful, consistent, and loving, they are more likely to be psychologically resilient as well.

There are three other well-known parenting styles: authoritarian, permissive, and uninvolved.

I'll briefly explain the other three in order to give you more context:

- Authoritarian parenting is "tyrannical." It focuses on having high expectations, very little affection, strict rules, and hard punishments.
- Permissive parenting is very affectionate. However, parents spoil the child to the point where it becomes unhealthy, giving in to their every whim.
- Uninvolved parenting is basically what the name says: uninvolved. This parenting style is often referred to as being neglectful.

When you think about the different parenting styles, it makes us consider things in a different light. You may not have noticed before that you have a certain parenting style. Some people combine the different types as well.

SETTING ROUTINES

Routines should be stable and predictable. Just like having a stable parent or authority figure helps kids in even the most unstable environments, so will a routine. When there are set morning and bedtime routines—perhaps even a weekend routine, that gives children a safety net. Regardless of what may happen, they know they can count on this routine to be there and to be consistent.

Setting up healthy routines are not as difficult as some make them sound. It can feel a little overwhelming at first, especially when you don't have much structure in your life, but it's possible.

A routine doesn't need to be intricate; it can be simple. If your children are younger, it's a good idea to have routines set up where they can see them, written in clear and age-appropriate language. If they can't read yet, use pictures.

I'll add a few sample routines to help you craft your very own. The first ones will be aimed at younger children who can read.

TIME	ACTIVITY	CHECKED YES/NO
6:00 AM	Wake up and have a glass of milk.	
6:10 AM	Brush teeth and comb hair.	
6:20 AM	Get dressed and put on your shoes.	
6:40 AM	Have breakfast.	
7:00 AM	Put a lunch box in your school bag.	
7:10 AM	Leave for school.	

TIME	ACTIVITY	CHECKED YES/NO
2:00 PM	School ends.	
2:20 PM	Get picked up from school.	
2:30 PM	Unpack school bag and put dirty laundry in the laundry bag.	
2:50 PM	Have a snack.	
3:10 PM	Have playtime.	
4:00 PM	Do homework.	
5:00 PM	Rest or play.	
6:00 PM	Wash up for dinner.	
6:10 PM	Have dinner.	
7:00 PM	Take a bath.	
7:30 PM	Have story time.	
8:00 PM	Go to bed.	

For children who cannot read yet, as mentioned, pictures can be used.

TIME	ACTIVITY	CHECKED YES/NO
6:00 AM	Wake up.	
6:10 AM	Brush your teeth and comb your hair.	
6:20 AM	Get dressed.	

TIME	ACTIVITY	CHECKED YES/NO
6:40 AM	Have breakfast.	
7:00 AM	Take your lunch box	
7:10 AM	Leave for school!	

TIME	ACTIVITY	CHECKED YES/NO
2:00 PM	School ends.	
2:20 PM	Get picked up from school.	
2:30 PM	Unpack school bag and put dirty laundry in the laundry basket.	

TIME	ACTIVITY	CHECKED YES/NO
2:50 PM	 Have a snack.	
3:10 PM	 Playtime.	
4:00 PM	 Do homework.	

TIME	ACTIVITY	CHECKED YES/NO
6:00 PM	Wash up for dinner.	
6:10 PM	Dinner time.	
7:00 PM	Take a bath.	

TIME	ACTIVITY	CHECKED YES/NO
7:30 PM	Have story time.	
8:00 PM	Go to bed.	

It's as simple as that. You can customize routines as much as you need to in order for them to suit your individual needs. Add chores, add more rest time, create weekend routines—whatever works. For older kids and teens, routines are still important. You can use the templates above for them as well. Simply add more detail and more advanced language. Routines can go on the fridge, on their bedroom door, or anywhere else where they see it frequently.

Aside from the strategies listed in this chapter, there are many other skills that your children can learn to help cultivate resilience. These will be the subject matter of the next chapter.

5

SKILLS THAT BUILD RESILIENCE

> Kids who feel overwhelmed or hopeless often won't attempt to address a problem. But when you give them a clear formula for solving problems, they'll feel more confident in their ability to try.
>
> —AMY MORIN, LCSW

U p until now, we have learned enough in terms of strategies; however, we are yet to get equipped with the mastery of a few essential skills. This chapter will guide us in honing three utmost skills that can help cultivate resilience in a child. We will further look into why such skills can affect the development of resilience and will finally discuss the Seven Cs of Resilience as proposed by child pediatrician Dr. Ginsburg.

COPING SKILLS

Coping skills are adaptive practical, and emotional strategies that assist us in dealing with stress and overcoming various challenges. They enable us to navigate difficult situations. Coping skills include diverse approaches such as problem-solving, seeking support, and reframing our perspective.

Without the crucial coping mechanisms we require, neither our children nor us would survive very long. Teaching our children healthy coping mechanisms is essential in helping them prepare for the adult life ahead of them. However, they need coping skills as kids and teens, too. We often underestimate everything they go through, including all the emotional changes and other challenges they face. Of course, to us, it may seem like nothing compared to adulthood, but to them, it's their reality and a big deal.

Examples of Healthy Coping Skills

- Deep breathing activities are helpful in many situations—from stressful or anxiety-inducing circumstances to anger-related situations. Younger children may not necessarily understand the concept of deep breathing, so we must explain it to them in age-appropriate ways. For example, say, "Take a seat and breathe in deeply, and when I have counted to five, stop and breathe out."

- Seeking support is a crucial coping skill, and we need to make sure they know where to go and who to turn to when they need help.

- Physical activity is good for stress relief and even helps relieve stress and depression. We can encourage our kids to play physical games and even play with them when we notice they may be undergoing a stressful situation.

- Mindfulness and meditation are healthy coping skills for all ages. However, it's not something that younger kids will necessarily understand. We can help them by teaching them about it in age-appropriate language and meditating with them. It won't be something all kids go along with, but you never know unless you try.

- Being creative helps kids express themselves. It is often used in therapy as well. Kids who have trouble communicating effectively might be asked to draw what they feel instead, which is a suitable coping mechanism for kids. It's not only for those who have trouble expressing themselves emotionally. Healthy kids can do this too. Encouraging creative outlets of any kind is beneficial.

- Effectively managing time is essential from a young age. Managing your time will definitely reduce stress. That's why structure is so important. We often forget that kids experience stress and anxiety like us, and setting routines brings familiarity and predictability.

Healthy Coping Skills That Can Help Younger Kids

- Journal or write short stories or poems.
- Sing soothing songs.
- Hug a pillow or stuffed animal, or literally—a tree.
- Play with pets or toys.
- Accompany parents on shopping trips.
- Play with Play-Doh.
- Build pillow forts.
- Dance in the living room.
- Make hot drinks such as hot chocolate with adult supervision.
- Plant a few seeds with the help of an adult.
- Watch happy movies or videos online.
- Take a hot shower or bath.
- Paint, draw, or get creative.
- Start a new collection or hobby.
- Let them cry if they need to cry.

Cultivating Resilience Through Healthy Coping Skills

"Research has shown that children can learn and develop new coping skills, enhancing their ability to adapt to challenging situations" (Frydenberg et al., 2021).

These coping resources as well as learned resourcefulness play a crucial role in shaping children's responses to stress. We can empower them to manage emotions, solve problems, seek support, and maintain a positive mindset.

Through the development of coping strategies, children can further build resilience, enabling them to face life's challenges with confidence, resourcefulness, and a positive outlook.

It's important to have all the pieces of the puzzle. You may teach your child to be resilient, you're a good role model, and you try and do everything you can to help; however, they may still struggle because they don't necessarily have the coping skills they need. It's like a chair with its legs; you need every leg to function properly.

EMOTION REGULATION AND MANAGEMENT

Managing or regulating emotions is about understanding, acknowledging, and effectively responding to one's emotions. It is about recognizing and accepting feelings and using strategies to modulate and channel them appropriately.

Whereas emotional control, on the other hand, is the capacity to suppress or restrain emotional reactions. Think about a bottle of soda. Controlling it is like shaking the bottle with the lid tightly screwed on. The problem is that the bottle will overflow and create a giant mess once you unscrew the cap. Firstly, it would be best not to shake the bottle;

however, life shakes us sometimes. In this case, the best way to deal with the shaking would be to slowly unscrew the lid, carefully letting the "anger" out not to create a big mess. We deal with it bit by bit, breaking it into smaller pieces, and we work through it instead of letting it blow out of proportion.

Emotional control is about keeping the outward expression of emotions calm (Raypole, 2020). However, the storm brewing inside is typically much more intense. Holding in emotions is not a healthy way to cope with intense emotions in the long run. Sure, we need to be able to restrain ourselves for short periods of time. For example, your child might need to bite their tongue in class if an educator treated them badly, but not over a long time. We need to ensure that our kids know this. They need to know that they are allowed to show their emotions and explain how they feel.

Managing or regulating is the best solution because it is more than just suppression.

Rather than suppressing or ignoring emotions, one should process and express them healthily and appropriately. This is what we should be encouraging in our children.

Again, emotions and feelings need to be acknowledged and validated. Help them describe their feelings and encourage them to reflect on what might be causing any of the emotions they may be experiencing. For example, if they've fought with a friend over something, help them recognize sadness, disappointment, or whatever else they may be feeling. That's not a bad thing. By assisting them to realize how they feel and why they are feeling it, we're also cultivating a sense of trust and a deeper bond. We can also help children identify their emotional triggers to assist them with managing their reactions. We also need to teach them techniques, such as the ones in the bulleted list above, to help them calm down. Remember, they will more likely do what they see us doing.

The right kind of emotional regulation and management will help our kids be more resilient in the face of failures and all the ups and downs of life. If they can process and regulate their feelings accordingly, they can easily overcome obstacles thrown at them, as resilience becomes easier with the proper management of emotions. Hence, our kids will be more likely to be empathetic towards themselves and others, and their emotional intelligence and self-control will speak for themselves.

Let's consider an example. For privacy, all names are once again changed to fictional ones.

Clarissa was thirteen years old and filled with intense emotions. It was always clear as day when she was upset, and she used to get extremely upset over what other children would consider to be small things. It was only a short time before Clarissa was one of the girls in the class with very few friends. She had trouble regulating her emotions, leading to anger and tears outbursts.

There came a day when she dropped her little plastic pencil sharpener from her desk. Before she could pick it up, one of her classmates accidentally stepped on it, causing a complete meltdown from Clarissa. This is a prime example of her inability to regulate her emotions effectively. What can also be learned from this story is that what others see as a minor misfortune could be a huge deal for someone else. This does not mean that a complete meltdown is the appropriate way to react. It is just some food for thought.

Her life had been tough from a young age. Growing up, she had an even more difficult time because she had never been taught the proper strategies to regulate emotions. It did not get any easier in adulthood. From work to romantic relationships, she could not keep anything.

It's a very unfortunate story, but it happens all the time. There doesn't have to be any underlying mental health issues for such a thing to occur. Any children who don't know the strategies may have similar issues. In childhood, parents and other family members may be able to help children deal with these problems; however, adulthood will be challenging.

A scenario like Clarissa's can be avoided if we are thorough and consistent with our guidance.

PROBLEM-SOLVING SKILLS

Problem-solving skills contribute to resilience by enabling children to approach challenges with a proactive and solution-oriented mindset. Problem-solving skills also teach children to think critically and creatively. They learn to think outside the box. This kind of thinking is invaluable in building resilience.

When children successfully solve problems, it boosts their belief in their ability to overcome those "lemons" that life so graciously throws at them. This helps form a foundation for resilience.

Problem-solving also dramatically helps the growth mindset that they so desperately need. They learn that mistakes and setbacks are a natural part of the problem-solving process and do not get discouraged easily.

As parents, we can help them develop their problem-solving skills by involving them in simple tasks such as arranging the pantry. This may sound far-fetched, but think about it. You have a large bag of flour, eggs, and other items. The top shelf of the pantry might not be so sturdy. There might be better ideas than placing a heavy bag of flour on there. They need to think critically to organize items in a way that works.

There are many other things you can do to help them develop their critical thinking and problem-solving skills. Puzzles and games such as chess are an excellent start for any child. While some may not enjoy it from the get-go, they may become quite fond of it with time. You can even involve them in some of your own problems.

Let's say that you sorted a budget of $300 for groceries on a shopping trip. Let them help keep calculations and choose cost-effective options to stretch your budget as far as possible. The possibilities are endless. We don't always realize how easily we can help kids develop all kinds of skills simply by involving them in our everyday lives.

Another great example is taking problems or situations that are more complex and teaching them how to break them into smaller, more manageable sections. Let's say your child has a big project for school, and looking at the project outline makes their head spin. Get a few colored pens and help them draw lines under a few points, marking milestones. This allows them to see a whole group of smaller goals to reach instead of one large chunk of work. Even household chores could be broken down. The ability to critically analyze a task and break it up is an invaluable skill.

Some kids may prefer doing things differently, and that's okay! Encourage them to try different approaches and learn from their experiences—whether the outcomes are successful.

"Possessing proficiency to deal with adversity and problem-solving tasks is considered critical to have resilient attitudes. Therefore, resiliency is the ability of individuals to use available personal and contextual resources to manage adversities" (De Almientoz Santos & Soares, 2018).

Connor-Davidson Resilience Scale

Believe it or not, there is actually a specific test that measures your level of resilience. It's called the Connor-Davidson Resilience Scale. It was first introduced by Kathryn M. Connor and Jonathan R.T. Davidson (Riopel, 2019).

The scale measures the following, as stated in an article on PositivePsychology.com, written by Leslie Riopel (2019).

- The ability to adapt to change.
- The ability to deal with what comes along.
- The ability to cope with stress.
- The ability to stay focused and think clearly.
- The ability to not get discouraged in the face of failure.
- The ability to handle unpleasant feelings such as anger, pain or sadness.

The scale was first designed due to their patients suffering from PTSD (Riopel, 2019). There are different versions of the test, each with their own unique characteristics. It originally had 25 items.

According to Riopel, there are only three versions that are said to be in legal use. The CD-RISC-2 is a relatively short version that only assesses two aspects of the scale: the ability to adapt when faced with changes and the ability to recover swiftly after experiencing adversities.

The CD-RISC-10 version is more comprehensive. It uses ten items instead of two. For the sake of brevity, we won't name all ten. It was developed and made popular by Dr. Campbell-Sills (Riopel, 2019).

The third one is CD-RISC-25, which is the original Connor-Davidson resilience scale, using 25 items to measure resilience.

The scoring is simple. People with the highest scores are said to be more resilient. I recommend that you go ahead and do some research on these. It's not only interesting to test yourself, but useful as well.

Dr. Ginsburg's Seven Cs of Resilience

Aside from the three skills already mentioned—coping, emotional management, and problem solving, there are seven other integral components and characteristics of resilience as proposed by child pediatrician, Dr. Ginsburg (CBT Professionals, 2013). It's important to note that these components are interconnected and reinforce one another. When you look at these seven facts, they reinforce what we've been discussing thus far.

1. *Competence* is the development of skills and a sense of being skilled at different things in their lives.
2. *Confidence* is their self-esteem—how children see themselves and how confident they are in their own abilities.

3. *Connection* is all about positive relationships discussed earlier on.

4. *Character* encompasses the development of integrity, a strong set of values, and a sense of responsibility.

5. *Contribution* involves helping children develop a sense of purpose and encouraging them to make a positive impact on the people around them.

6. *Coping* refers to the ability to manage stress, regulate emotions, and cope effectively with challenges. We've already discussed the importance of coping skills in cultivating resilience.

7. *Control* involves empowering children to recognize that they have control over their own choices, actions, and responses to situations.

Each of these directly connects to fostering resilience in our children.

The Seven Cs of Resilience are widely known; however, people easily overlook them. Today, I want to challenge you to look at them and see how you can use them to help your life and the lives of your children.

Look at different activities that can help develop each of these, and place emphasis on the importance they carry.

What You Can Do to Help Your Child With Each "C"

COMPETENCE

Support them in everything they do. Be that parent who shows up at the sporting event with war paint and a team shirt. Encourage them to work hard for what they want without focusing on their failures. Help them focus on growth instead.

Take a few minutes each day to practice a specific skill your child may have trouble with—reading, math, drawing, or something else. Let them practice and track their progress to show them how far they have come. You'll see their confidence shoot sky high along with their competence.

CONFIDENCE

Once they become more confident, they will become more competent in different aspects of their lives. Don't be afraid to let them participate in all kinds of activities. Unless they prefer it that way, they don't have to be wall flowers.

An excellent example of how you can cultivate confidence in children is to remind them of their "wins." You don't want to be overbearing, but if they're struggling with a specific task, it is good to say, "Remember when you thought you wouldn't make the team, and you did? You can do this!" This encourages them to work hard and reminds them of obstacles they've previously overcome.

CONNECTION

What you can do as a family to build connections is to ensure that you spend enough time together. When a family spends quality time together, they form deeper connections. Remember, the first deep and important connection they form as small children is with their immediate family.

What it means to spend quality time together differs from what we usually think. For example, watching movies together is not quality time spent together. It's sitting together, sure, but there is the probability that no deeper connection is being fostered. Hence, you have to be present and indulge in meaningful discussions, too, even if you just ask them about their day. Play a board game, build a puzzle, or even build blocks together. With activities such as these, you're communicating with each other and working together to achieve something.

CHARACTER

Kids are unfortunately susceptible to peer pressure and all the latest trends—especially teenagers. We often see hurtful pranks on social media, and kids conduct themselves riskily because their peers see it as acceptable behavior. They usually don't consider that they're hurting themselves or someone else. This is a bad character. Having open and hard discussions about these things is a good place to start. We must ensure our kids know the difference between right and wrong. Remember to celebrate diversity and individuality as much as possible to help our children realize that it's okay to be your own person and that being different isn't bad.

CONTRIBUTION

Encourage your kids to be kind to their peers and volunteer for any community work they can—perhaps at a local animal shelter or soup kitchen or helping keep the school grounds clean. No matter the contribution, helping in any capacity is a win.

COPING

Remember some tips above regarding coping skills, such as journaling and seeking support from trusted family members or friends. Support them as much as you can. Sometimes, even knowing the finest coping skills, a kid needs a hug from a loving parent.

CONTROL

Emphasize the fact that their choices are their own. They can choose to skip school but are not free of the consequences. Remind them that they are in control of how they react to situations and treat others.

Resilience, as you know by now, is a critical skill to have in life. However, circumstances are sometimes uniquely challenging, and cultivating resilience may be complex. That doesn't mean it isn't possible, and that's what we'll be looking at in the next chapter.

CHAPTER 6

BUILDING RESILIENCE UNDER SPECIAL CIRCUMSTANCES

"Two tensions were found to impede resilience: social justice and power and control" (Wilcox, L., Larson, K., & Bartlett, R., 2021).

DEVELOPING RESILIENCE IN CHILDREN WHO FACE SPECIAL circumstances is an uphill task but not an impossibility. Special circumstances don't necessarily mean your kids will be negatively impacted for life, and there is no going beyond it. In this chapter, we will explore how those severely affected by negative eventualities can be assisted in attaining resilience. We will discuss Adverse Childhood Experiences (ACEs) and how these can affect a child's resilience.

MORE INTENSE CHALLENGES

It is a fact that some children will face more challenges than others. They may encounter prejudice, bias, and unfair treatment simply because of who they are or due to the circumstances they were born into. They face daily challenges due to class, race, social position, and religion. To be resilient in the face of such prejudice, discrimination, and bias is not exactly an easy task; however, it's not insurmountable either.

When you think about it logically, seeing a failure as a learning experience can be very complicated if you don't have a proper support system or fail more frequently than you succeed—especially if the failure is due to factors beyond your control. In such scenarios, kids are particularly vulnerable to the mindset of *Why me?* That's a question that some of us may get asked, and it isn't easy to answer. It's important to note that you don't always need to have all the answers—even if you're a parent. Don't pretend to know; it's okay to tell them that you don't know the answer to this particular question and that we may never know. But we can reassure them that whatever challenges they face will make them more resilient and that they are special regardless of the circumstances.

It isn't easy to foster a growth mindset or any kind of positivity if kids are focused on what they perceive as more important in the short term than in the long run. These could include things we take for granted, such as having a cooked meal or school supplies. Hence, they must think in a long-term frame as it can affect their future choices.

In this chapter, I will discuss a few categories of children who may find it more challenging to develop resilience than others. It is also important to note that there are many more categories of children who face unique circumstances; however, we'll only focus on three:

- children with special needs
- children with diverse backgrounds
- children with adverse childhood experiences

Remember that these categories are not exhaustive or exclusive, and other groups of children also face unique challenges.

SPECIAL NEEDS

"A special needs child is a youth who has been determined to require special attention and specific necessities that other children do not" (Kagan, 2019).

Some children need a little more support in their journey to adulthood than others, like kids with special needs. This means they need a little extra help, a bit of an extra lift, to develop resilience. Nothing prevents special needs children from being just as resilient as other children as long as they are adequately supported. Resilience is not limited to particular individuals or circumstances; rather, it is a quality that can be nurtured and developed in all children—including those with special needs.

One of the most vital keys to developing resilience is having a supportive and inclusive environment that acknowledges and celebrates one's strengths. A child with special needs will not likely thrive if they do not have the support they deserve.

An important thing to consider in this regard is the school that you choose for them. Some children with special needs have the means of going to schools that are specially equipped to educate them, and there they feel more at ease as they don't feel like outcasts.

Sometimes, it's not always possible for a child to attend a special needs school, and they may have trouble flourishing in a standard school. Even if they do well academically, kids around them can be mean. Bullies will go as far as to bully a child with special needs.

In such a case, resilience becomes more important than ever, and they will undoubtedly need your support. Coping skills are also crucial at this stage because they help build emotional strength. It's natural that our special needs children might have difficulty navigating the ups and downs of growing up; however, we can help them by nurturing healthy coping skills just like the ones we've previously discussed.

Mental Health

Let's take a child with autism spectrum disorder (ASD) who has trouble with social interactions. The school could become nearly unbearable for such children if they are not nurtured in the right direction. In such a case, you could help the child by encouraging them to try activities that teach social skills.

My best advice is to find support groups with like-minded people. Playdates can be organized where children can practice their social skills while being supervised.

As another example, children with ADHD may need special care with their academic work, time management, and procrastination. They may need special permission for things such as fidget toys. These are accommodations that can be arranged with the school. You'll want to ensure that the educators tasked with teaching your child are also accepting and supportive.

Physical Disabilities

Children who have physical disabilities can be susceptible to bullying, and you need to make sure that they are comfortable with speaking to you about it. They also need to know that they can still reach great heights even if they might be limited. You might want to offer frequent praise and encouragement; however, no matter how tempting it is to want to help them with everything, they need to be able to work on their independence as well. Encourage them to try things they can do themselves and practice things they might not be able to do themselves just yet. A good balance is important. Show them they are not disabled; instead, consider using the term "differently abled."

Every child is unique; not one of them has the same limitations or talents as another. Special needs children are no different. They have interests and skills just like anyone else.

Other Helpful Tips

As mentioned before, involving the school and collaborating with educators is good. Teachers spend more time with our kids than we do at some points, so it's only natural that they would have a powerful effect on their mental development and overall well-being.

Collaborating with the educators involved in your child's everyday life will undoubtedly set them up for success. A positive relationship with a trusted teacher can be just as important as a positive relationship with a family member. Moreover, it also offers additional stability from which all children benefit; the stability of an adult figure they can count on in times of distress.

At school, some helpful activities and strategies can be put in place to assist special needs children:

- wheelchair accessibility
- special allowances for body breaks
- special allowances for fidget toys
- a teacher that checks up regularly and offers additional support
- changing up games so that special needs children can also take part in them
- motivational speakers to educate other students
- courses offered to educate teachers on how to help and teach special needs children
- raising awareness within the community
- ensuring that special needs children are included in activities at school

This list is not exhaustive, and a whole mountain of other things can be done to help further the cause. Some schools may not have the means to make it happen, but some are absolutely attainable. As a parent, you can advocate for all special needs children, including yours. You can also help by being involved with some of these activities, such as raising awareness.

By supporting our special needs children, we can help them cultivate the resilience they need. Offering them additional support will not diminish their resilience, and the idea that they need to learn to "figure things out on their own" is not healthy. That is an important fact to keep in mind.

SPREADING THE SEEDS OF RESILIENCE

> "A good half of the art of living is resilience."
>
> **—ALAIN DE BOTTON**

The resilience of our children is something most of us worry about as parents. Stress hits the upcoming generations faster and harder than it did ours. The modern world is fast-paced and busy, and there's already a lot of pressure coming at kids before they even reach the stage of life where they have a career and a family to think about. We don't just want them to be prepared to handle the future; we want them to be able to handle the present moment with strength and resilience.

Both my career and my own life experience have shown me the value of developing resilience at a young age and how it shapes our success in the future, and it's because of this that I'm so passionate about sharing this information with as many parents as possible. I know how big a concern this is for parents, and my challenge now is helping them to find the guidance they're looking for – and that's where you come in.

As I'm sure you know yourself, the experience of other parents and their children is a huge asset on the parenting journey, and we're all looking to collect all the inspiration we can. So if you'd be willing to take a few moments to write a short review, you'll help other parents find what they're looking for and trust that they're hitting on resources that have helped other families.

By leaving a review of this book on Amazon, you'll show other parents who want to ensure their children have all the resilience they need to build a life of happiness and success exactly where they can find the guidance they're looking for.

Every parent wants to know that they're doing the right thing for their children, and when they're looking for information, they want to be sure that it's information other parents trust.

Thank you so much for your support. Together, we can help strengthen the confidence and resiliency of a whole generation.

To Leave a Review, scan the QR Code.

Additional Challenges Faced

"Young people with a learning difficulty may also be at increased risk of substance misuse, which Cosden (2001) suggests may be a negative coping strategy related to the developmental need for family support over a longer period of time, increased difficulty in making friendships with peers, and a lack of understanding of the effects of their own disability" (Hart et al., 2016).

It's important to note that children with special needs may face higher risks of "falling off the wagon." They can easily fall into the wrong habits without the resilience they require to face life's challenges. Such habits can involve substance abuse, vigorous gaming, or frequently accessing adult content online. All these apparent escapes are unhealthy coping mechanisms, which is why healthy coping strategies are so vital.

Understanding Their Condition

Before we consider anything else, we do need to ensure that we fully understand whatever particular condition the child may have. To support them to the best of our abilities, we need to fully comprehend the extent of their skills and possible limitations. If we hope to cultivate resilience in children with special needs, we need to think realistically.

Sometimes, certain things cannot be adjusted to accommodate special needs children. In such cases, we need to be upfront with them. However, being upfront does not mean being cold. We must deliver messages gently from a place of care and love.

For example, if a child who cannot see wants to be a proficient cursive writer. With a lot of practice and support, it might be possible; however, the odds might be a little stacked against him/her. In such a case, it might be best, to be honest, yet remind them that just because one thing may not work out, it doesn't mean that others will not. Not everyone can do everything. If they fail, yet they've been raised to be resilient, they will absolutely bounce back and persevere.

Do as much research as you can to ensure that you help them set realistic goals. While we may see failure as an opportunity for growth, we don't want them to get hurt unnecessarily. We often want every child to reach beyond the stars, but some things are just unfeasible. For example, a child who has had their legs amputated may not be the number one swimmer in the world, but they can surely try and learn to swim. That in itself is a massive goal reached, and it is worth a celebration.

Similarly, encourage them to try new and more diverse activities. For example, a child who cannot see could still be a pianist. It's not about seeing; it's about feeling. He could be an artist, even if he cannot see his work. The brush strokes and thrill of creating art remain the same.

All in all, the outlook is a positive one. There is always light at the end of the tunnel, and your child is bound to reach their dreams with suitable support, realistic goals, and resilience. The sky is the limit!

DIVERSE BACKGROUNDS

Talking about different backgrounds has gained a sensitive salience these days. Yet, it's something we do need to talk about. You might be a parent reading this, an educator, or someone who can significantly impact the lives of children around you. Remember the positive relationships we spoke about? You could be that positive person for someone.

Not every child has the same opportunities. Race and background, unfortunately, do play a role in that—even in this modern age. For this reason, children with diverse backgrounds have a pronounced need to be resilient.

Do you remember the story of the girl I told in the introduction who moved away from her country of origin? It was a tough time for her. She had a diverse background and moved to a whole new world with very little to begin with. Resilience got her through it, and it can also get others through it. She came from an entirely different culture, and suddenly, she was shocked by new things: people, languages, and so much more. It felt surreal. No matter where we grow up, we typically learn about other cultures through stories or by genuinely living among them. However, getting to experience a different culture firsthand and then having the ability to adapt to it are two distinct processes.

Common Challenges Faced

One of the biggest challenges children with diverse backgrounds often face is language. We don't always think about it; we speak, and everyone around us speaks to us, and it's all easy. However, picture a child moving countries to a place where their mother tongue is not spoken, and they need to learn a new language. Learning the language may be only the beginning. They may face bullying because they do not understand concepts or because of their accents, among other things.

There is this incredibly nasty stigma that anyone who does not have one of the standard English accents does not have the same level of intelligence as others. In reality, intelligence cannot simply be measured as an accent or dialect.

Language is a product of culture. On our big green earth, we have a vast range of beautiful cultures. Each is unique in its way. The issue is that with so many different cultures and individual beliefs, some people may struggle to assimilate.

Let's take an American child who suddenly moves to an African country. While language may not be the biggest issue (since many people on the African continent do have an understanding of English), the cultural difference is quite substantial. The same can be said for a child raised in Africa who suddenly moves to the US. A lack of understanding of cultural traditions, backgrounds, and practices can be difficult to overcome.

Unfortunately, bullying is even more prevalent in these cases.

How Can We Help Them?

Whether you're a parent or an educator, the first thing you can do is ensure that the child you're trying to assist has adequate access to resources to help them learn about cultural and linguistic differences. This does not mean that they relinquish their own, but to be resilient and adapt to a new environment where they may be an underrepresented group, they need to learn about the new world before them.

By having access to the right resources, we're cultivating resilience in them, along with boosting their confidence level. If you send a Hispanic child who knows nothing about Canada to a Canadian school with nothing but a uniform and a lunch box, chances are they will have tremendous trouble adapting. Now, if you arm them with a translation app, some videos, and books about interesting cultural and historical facts, they'll probably have an easier time adjusting.

When we examine resilience from a broader perspective, we uncover not only the unequal distribution of resources but also the existing structural disadvantages that already exist, like racial marginalization, which present particular challenges for some people or groups. This understanding demonstrates how systemic barriers and societal factors, which can disproportionately affect certain populations, also have an impact on resilience.

The Importance of Recognition

"When adults acknowledge and appreciate children's efforts and abilities, it enhances their resilience as learners. However, it has been mentioned that younger children from minority ethnic groups in the classroom were less likely to receive this kind of recognition compared to older children. This lack of recognition directly affected the levels of resilience in these children. Resilience is seen as a back-and-forth interaction between a child and their social and cultural environment, so when children don't receive recognition, it can have a negative impact on their ability to bounce back from challenges and setbacks" (Chowbey & Barley, 2022).

We've previously emphasized the importance of striking a balance when appreciating and praising children. Praise is necessary throughout the journey as learning an entirely new culture, language, and maybe more isn't easy. Children who try to adapt need to be recognized for their efforts to do so.

I believe the problem arises when people see children as *more* adaptable—especially if they're still in their formative years. It should be easier to soak up what is around them, correct? Well, that's not entirely true. We need to ensure that their efforts are well received and recognized and that they feel confident in their ability to adapt. Don't ever take this for granted; not because your child is small, they will adapt more quickly.

How Do You Nurture Resilience in Kids From Diverse Backgrounds?

Talk about it. The difficulties children from diverse backgrounds experience go beyond those we've already mentioned. Injustice may cross their paths much more than we would like it to. The first thing we can do to help them is to talk about it. Don't let them be silenced. Let them speak to you or other supportive figures in their lives. Once the discussion has begun, it can change the attitudes and hence perceptions.

Let them speak out. It's good to nurture a spirit of resilience by encouraging them to speak out against injustice. Even if your child is not necessarily the one with a very diverse background, teach them to speak out against what they know to be wrong. Help them help others. Nurture in them the values of uprightness and justice.

Encourage safe risks. A child may be scared if he is about to enter a new world they don't know. Naturally, they might be hesitant to attend the year's first school dance or participate in the athletics team. Don't let that fear get in their way.

Encourage them to do what makes them happy and to face those healthy risks with their heads held high.

Turn the other cheek. Cultivating kindness and tolerance should not be taken for granted; it is necessary to build a compassionate character. In order to foster resilience, we need to teach them not to dwell on insults or bullies. Sometimes, one cannot reason with someone, and they may attempt to make your child's life difficult. To not let their spirit be broken, your child needs to learn to "shake it off" and, quite literally, be the "bigger person." When they indulge bullies by trying to slander them back or by trying to argue their way out of a fight, all they're doing is upsetting themselves further. However, we need to be cautious not to sound dismissive to their upset feelings when they express them.

If you're an educator, you are in a better position to help these children. You frequently get to witness things that most parents do not. You can do your part by speaking out against bullying and making sure that your classroom, at the very least, is a safe space. You can also educate other students on cultural differences and acceptance.

Every educator must understand that bullying is abnormal and cannot be reduced to childhood rivalries. It needs to be addressed every time and should not be ignored. I am aware that this may place educators in a difficult position—especially when they may need to involve parents—but for the sake of the students, it's crucial to do so—not only to help the child being bullied but also to help the bully understand why their behavior is not acceptable, regardless of what they may be going through.

As a parent, you can raise your kids to be tolerant and kind—whether they're the new kids in a strange new world or vice versa.

Nurturing resilience in children from diverse backgrounds is similar to nurturing resilience in any child. You just may need to tweak a few things here and there.

Both parents and educators need to be aware of anti-bullying resources in their district or community, and there are many.

ADVERSE CHILDHOOD EXPERIENCES

ACEs are events or situations during childhood that can have a negative impact on a child's well-being and development (Herzog & Schmahl, 2018). These experiences can vary, but they all share the potential to affect a child's life in significant ways.

ACEs, including bullying, can significantly affect a child's psychological development in various ways. Mentally, they may experience increased anxiety, depression, or difficulty concentrating. Psychologically, ACEs can lead to low self-esteem and a lack of boundaries. Emotionally, they may struggle to regulate their emotions, leading to frequent outbursts or emotional withdrawal.

Other types of ACEs that may hinder a child's development:

- Abusive family members—including sexual, verbal, and physical abuse
- Witnessing the abuse of others by family members
- Divorce—especially if it is not what we call a "clean" divorce
- The death of loved ones
- Neglect and abandonment

There are many others, but these are some common ones also discussed in an article on the Integrative Life Center website called "What Are the 10 Adverse Childhood Experiences" published in 2021.

ACEs hinder the development of skills necessary for building resilience. They can undermine the process by creating obstacles that make it harder for children to develop these necessary skills. For instance, if a child has experienced chronic neglect, they may struggle to form secure attachments with others, which is crucial for resilience. This can cut them from having positive relationships that are very beneficial for fostering resilience.

Children who have experienced trauma or adversity may face increased difficulties in managing stress, problem-solving, and seeking support. Their previous negative experiences can create barriers to building healthy coping mechanisms and trusting relationships, which, as you know, are the hallmarks of resilience.

As adults, we play a vital role in teaching children to be resilient, especially in the aftermath of ACEs. Everything we've discussed thus far plays just as much of a significant role as creating a safe space and encouraging open communication in order to help them heal and cultivate resilience.

ACE's need to be understood and managed as soon as possible to avoid further issues later into adulthood. It's not uncommon for ACEs to affect nearly every aspect of an adult's life.

> Let them not fail before their lives have even begun.
>
> **—AUTHOR UNKNOWN**

There is one thing I need you, Dear Reader, to take out of this: Resilience does not negate what you've been through. When it comes to resilience, there are many people whose strengths are overlooked because they appear to function just fine even after serious ACEs.

There is some stigma around ACEs in the sense of people stating things such as, "It must not have been that bad. They seem fine." While we're on this journey, something we need to remember—especially when it comes to our children—is that their feelings are valid, and what they went through matters.

Being resilient does not mean a person is indestructible. The world is too quick to make assumptions about successful people—whether it be a child with good grades or an adult with a successful career. People often assume that these thriving people must have "had it easy" or that their lives must not have been that bad.

> "Sometimes it is easier to be a victim; talking about how other people make you do what you do removes the obligation to change. And sympathy can feel sweet; talk of resilience can make some feel that no one is really appreciating exactly how much they have suffered" (Marano, 2003).

Making people feel this way is something that we try our best to avoid. A victim mindset is not ideal, but that does not mean their experiences are invalid.

ACEs affect children, but resilience helps them grow. A toxic past doesn't need to define them. Even if their family might not have a track record for resilience, we can change that. I believe that genetics may play a slight role, but in this case, the age-old argument of "nature versus nurture" comes into play. In the context of cultivating resilience, nurture is the winner.

Finding Resilience in Adversity

Nothing is quite like watching a child overcome obstacles and flourish into adulthood. I want to share a few stories to illustrate what we've discussed. We'll once again use "fictional names."

Chaney

Chaney was a young girl born into a poverty-stricken home. Nobody in her family had finished school; unfortunately, sexual abuse was present in her household. A woman I know recalled fondly the friendship she shared with young Chaney. However, her facial expression while recalling the story showed the grief that she felt for the girl while they were growing up.

The odds were completely stacked against Chaney. She was taken from her home and sent into foster care before high school. On school holidays, she was permitted to visit her grandmother—arguably the only positive influence she had in her family.

She dropped out of school and went down the wrong path. However, at the age of 20, she went back and got her high school diploma. She decided she would not be content working on a chicken farm like her mother and sleeping in one bedroom with five other family members. She was not okay with physical, mental, and sexual abuse.

She got a job and worked hard for everything she had. Eventually, she met a good man; today, she is a young, married, working woman. She lives in a big city. Even though the apartment may be small, it is hers. It's free of toxicity, and she rose above her family circumstances.

She credits the women who cared for her while she was in foster care and her grandmother for cultivating resilience in her and nurturing her in the right direction.

Martin

This next real-life example teaches us that it doesn't matter where you or your child come from, who your family is, or what has happened in their lives; everything can change in a day.

Martin was only seven years old when his parents got divorced. Unlike most children, he wasn't upset about it; in fact, He was quite happy about it. His parents had been in a very toxic relationship. He witnessed them fighting all his life, enduring the toxicity of a household marred by verbal abuse.

He grew afraid and withdrawn. However, when his parents split up, he had the opportunity to have two happy homes instead of one war zone.

The relationship his parents had affected most of his relationships as he grew older. He was not only emotionally scarred, but he also thought that their behavior was acceptable.

Around seven years later, Martin yelled at his girlfriend, humiliating her in front of the entire school, and then his parents realized the injustice they had done to their son. They did the right thing by having a stern conversation with him and making plans for therapy sessions.

Martin didn't realize his parents' influence on his life until he went into therapy and started delving deeper into his subconscious mind.

Despite the ACEs he faced, he overcame and received the help he needed from his mental health practitioners, supportive educators, and friends. His parents also sought therapy and got the help they needed. He now has two happy homes and still regularly goes for therapy sessions. His resilience shines through because he is strong enough to admit and take responsibility for his mistakes.

To sum up, resilience is a matter of teaching and supporting your child. It's not up to fate; it is up to you.

Another way children can find resilience in adversity is by fostering a strong sense of identity and purpose. We will consider the topsy and turvy journey into identity in the next chapter.

7

IDENTITY AND RESILIENCE

The United Nations recognizes children as capable members of society in their own right and that children can, and should, influence the world around them including the people they share it with (1989).

As social animals, we define ourselves in relation to society while simultaneously maintaining our unique personal identity. Identity, the way we perceive ourselves, plays a crucial role in building our self-hood and self-esteem. It starts to develop in childhood and reaches maturity in adulthood. The way a child perceives himself can impact the development of resilience. Hence, regardless of age, children should be given opportunities and resources to explore their identity and autonomy.

THEIR IDENTITY

One of the core components of who we are as people is our identity. It includes our attitudes toward ourselves and other people, as well as our beliefs, values, and interests. As parents, we significantly impact how well our kids navigate the challenging process of self-discovery and identity formation. Identity can be described in two ways: social identity and personal identity—also known as self-identity. Social identity refers to the groups or categories we belong to, such as gender, ethnicity, nationality, or religion. These aspects of our identity are shaped by the social and cultural contexts in which we grow up and interact. On the other hand, personal identity makes each of us distinct. For example, the combination of traits, values, and experiences that make each person a unique individual.

There is no age for children to begin exploring who they are. They absorb and get significantly influenced by the people and places around them. We must encourage them to ask questions and make them comfortable to express themselves without judgment.

One way to nurture their identity development is by exposing them to diverse experiences and perspectives. For example, you can read books that depict characters from different backgrounds, celebrate cultural traditions, or engage in activities that promote empathy and understanding of others. Even if we don't necessarily agree with certain cultural or religious views, we can still learn about them. This not only cultivates their appreciation for diversity but also helps them learn and form a significant portion of their identity.

It won't be long until they begin asking themselves questions about who they are, who they want to be, and what they believe in. We shouldn't discourage this. It's an unavoidable part of growing up. In truth, some people struggle with their identity until well into adulthood or beyond. To avoid such a predicament, let them explore and try new things, and let them know that they are safe and welcome to share their opinions respectfully.

I know it can be hard to accept that your child might be completely different from you, but that's the thing: they are not you. If we've been raised a certain way, it's tempting to want to raise our kids the same. This doesn't relate to parenting styles but more to religion, culture, traditions, and more. In truth, we can teach them everything we were taught, and we should, but we can't force our identities on them for long. When they're older, they will decide who they want to be, and within reason, we shouldn't become an obstacle in their way.

Many movies feature parents who force their dreams onto their children. For example, a mother wants to be a famous dancer, but it doesn't work out. What does she do? She forces her daughter into dancing lessons for years and is too harsh on her. One thing these movies have in common is that the situation blows up and creates a crater between parent and child; the child eventually decides their own course. Finally, the parent either accepts them or is depicted as the villain. Which one would you rather be? Don't get me wrong, I know in certain situations, we will stand our ground and not agree with their choices. We must do this in love.

As children go through different stages of development, their identities may evolve and go through constant flux. It's essential to be flexible and supportive during these transitions. Encourage them to embrace their growth and empower them to make choices that align with their authentic selves.

How Can We Help Our Children Find Their Identities?

The most important thing to remember is to be present and be accepting of them. Though experimentation is crucial for self-discovery, we still need to set boundaries to contain it within the limits of reason.

An excellent first step in this regard can be educating our children about the dangers of certain things, as some things ought not be experimented with. For example, when it comes to substance abuse, some illicit drugs need only be used once or twice for addiction to take hold (KidsHealth Behavioral Health Experts, 2018).

Like illicit drugs, underage drinking, and other harmful activities need to be avoided as they possess the potency to shape habits. Let's face it: most teenagers will probably find a way to do what you told them not to do. That's why we help them by not being the authoritarian parent who threatens them with punishment; instead, we help them by thoroughly and empathetically educating them.

What does this have to do with helping them find their identities? We must ensure that they are in the loop while experimenting and trying new things to figure out who they are, not straying.

Another way in which we can help them is by encouraging them to reflect on their behavior, values, and self. As mentioned, trends and fads are all over, and our children are susceptible to them. Do they really like cats? Or do they like cats because their teen idol does? That's a silly example, but it conveys the crux. It challenges them to question their likes and dislikes and analyze whether they truly feel a certain way. They are on the bandwagon of social influence.

Normalize asking them questions that make them think about deeper reasons. That said, remember that the journey of finding one's identity is subjective and unique for everyone. As parents, we can provide a supportive and nurturing environment that allows our children to explore, question, and embrace who they are. With guidance, validation, and acceptance, we can help our children develop an authentic sense of self-identity.

However, where validation is essential for a child, the excess of it can foster a sense of entitlement. Nowadays, it's very typical for people to anticipate that their family, parents, and society at large would accept them exactly as they are without even having an opinion on it; as a result, we are not permitted to disagree with our children unless we want to be branded the enemy.

I feel strongly that we need to unlearn this and reestablish this understanding in our kids—that we do not have to fully agree with them or approve of whatever they want all the time. As parents, it is part of our job to say "No" when necessary. As much as our kids have the right to be different, we also have the right to disagree with them.

We can also help them by allowing them autonomy (within reason). This tip is helpful in many cases. Encouraging independence in children fosters their personal growth and development and builds their confidence and self-esteem. By gradually increasing their responsibilities, such as completing household chores or making decisions, they learn valuable life skills and become more capable individuals. Additionally, facing and overcoming challenges independently can help children conquer their fears and develop resilience, preparing them for future obstacles they may encounter.

Consider the following example:

You live on a farm, and your little child fears chickens. You could simply keep them away from the chickens, or you could ask them to accompany you when feeding the chickens. Or you could pick one up and bring it to them so they can feel their feathers' softness. While you're at it, bring some humor into it by moving the chicken around, showing them how their heads stay still no matter how you move their bodies. For those who don't know, it's hilarious! Look it up.

This playful interaction with the chickens will not only help your child overcome their fear by associating them with positive experiences, but it can also teach them about the different behaviors and characteristics of animals, fostering their curiosity and love for nature.

Tip:

For a child, finding their identity is like building a brand-new house with four essential components. Imagine that each component represents an important aspect of who you are and how you develop.

The first one is their personal characteristics, which are the foundation. The second one is your family, which can be compared to the walls of the house. The third is their school, which represents the rooms inside the house. And finally, the fourth one is their social environment, similar to the neighborhood surrounding the house.

Just like a house needs all these components to be sturdy and complete, their identity is shaped by the combination of your personal characteristics, family, school, and social environment.

How Does Establishing an Identity Impact the Resilience-building Process?

Our children's sense of identity provides a solid basis for confronting challenges and overcoming obstacles. It's important to know who you are to be as resilient as you need to be. Of course, kids and teens don't know who they are yet, but their core beliefs and values are set from a young age. It's rare to come across someone who, for example, once could not stand animal abuse in childhood but suddenly doesn't mind it in adulthood.

Understanding their strengths, weaknesses, values, and interests helps children to better recognize their emotions, cope with stress, and make decisions that align with their authentic selves (Sutton, 2020).

Establishing an identity also contributes to the development of a sense of purpose in children's lives. This helps them to set meaningful goals, stay motivated during difficult times, and find purpose in their actions (Steger et al., 2021).

A strong identity also plays a pivotal role in establishing positive relationships. When children have a clear sense of self, they can form genuine connections based on shared values and interests (Pillow et al., 2015).

In a nutshell, identity development is a critical component of the resilience-building process in children. It empowers them to navigate challenges, develop confidence, find purpose, build meaningful relationships, and embrace diversity.

THEIR PURPOSE

Kids can explore their sense of purpose at any age because their interests motivate them, just like they can with their identity. A thorough vision of one's life goals, values, and aspirations is called a sense of purpose. The key is believing what you do matters and having a feeling of purpose and direction. An individual with a strong sense of purpose not only has a motivational drive but is inspired and finds greater fulfillment in his life and in all that he does.

How Can We Help Our Children Cultivate Their Sense of Purpose?

The truth of the matter is that we can try to help them when it comes to finding a sense of purpose, but we can't find it for them. At the end of the day, it is their life. What we can do, however, is guide and support them in their navigation. We are only the support crew on their life's ship, of which they are the captains. We are the advisory board, but we must not forget that they will make the final choices.

Their purpose in life—the thing that drives them every day—will likely not be the same as yours. You may be passionate about the environment, and that's wonderful, but your child might be more passionate about art or rescuing animals, and that's great too. Every person on this planet needs their own unique sense of purpose. Without it, some people may fall into a deep depression with a mindset of *Why am I even here?*

We're quick to want to preach about one thing or another, but this is a time to ask questions. If they show a genuine interest in something, ask them about it and help further their passion by being supportive.

You need to show genuine curiosity, even if a rock band isn't exactly what you're interested in. If their sense of purpose comes from creating the kind of music that would scare you and me off, then so be it. Share positivity and encourage them and let them know that the work they are putting in means something.

Take music, like we discussed above. Music can be used to raise awareness about anything, really. Politics, the environment, poverty, injustice: It can all be addressed with music. Other interests like writing, journaling, reading, and caring for others: All of it can be used for *more*.

The very best we can do is encourage them to go after what they want. Sometimes, they might just require a bit of a nudge into a direction—not helping or persuading—but nudging. By that I mean that it's good to expose them to different things and hobbies.

Take them to a museum, take them to a concert, take them to public speaking—anything that might "plant a seed" (Paulynice, 2020). Once that seed is planted, help them set short-term and long-term goals for themselves regarding these passions.

A short-term goal is something that can be attained in say, less than a year. Long-term goals are typically larger and require more than a year.

For example, if your child should find interest in animals, they can set the following goals:

SHORT-TERM GOALS	DATE ACHIEVED
Volunteer at an animal shelter nearby.	10 June, 2023
Collect ten bags of cat or dog food and ten blankets from donors for the shelter.	17 September, 2023
Catch as many stray cats or dogs as I can, take them to the shelter, and help them find good homes. Aim for ten animals.	20 December, 2023
Flea bath 20 dogs or cats at the shelter I volunteer at.	23 December, 2023

By setting short-term goals, they remain motivated throughout their journey, and these short-term goals can help lead them to long-term goals.

LONG-TERM GOALS	DATE ACHIEVED
Work at least part-time at the animal shelter after graduation.	2027
Go to college and study to be a vet.	2028
Obtain a degree.	2032
Begin first job as a vet.	2034
Open my own practice.	2040

Of course, these long-term goals are only an example. Someone interested in animals could also go on to open their animal shelter or be a vet's assistant. The point remains the same: Long-term goals are years away, and short-term goals keep you motivated along the way.

Since life doesn't always go our way, resilience will be helpful when setting goals like these. The course of life might take a different direction. Their interests may shift, or specific objectives may not be achievable due to external factors. Being resilient will enable them to overcome setbacks or failures they encounter along the way and assist them in creating new goals for themselves.

Does having a sense of purpose help build resilience? Absolutely! Will one or two failures bring your child down if they have a sincere goal and are committed to achieving it? No. They will get back up and try again because they want to reach a long-term pursuit. That right there is true resilience.

THEIR AUTONOMY

I want to bring up this topic once more because it is crucial to this journey. Children benefit from being encouraged to be independent because it helps them acquire essential life skills, self-reliance, and a sense of autonomy. They learn to take responsibility for their actions, learn from their mistakes, and hone their problem-solving skills. It's equally crucial to emphasize that being independent doesn't mean facing everything alone. Being mature enough to ask for help is not a sign of weakness but rather a sign of maturity.

Resilience lies in finding the balance between independence and asking for help. It's about teaching children to be resourceful and self-reliant while fostering an environment where seeking support is encouraged and valued.

Once again, we can tie this into having positive relationships. If they have positive relationships with people who positively influence them, they'll be more confident in asking for help when required.

Be careful not to focus too much on resilience that you forget that these are children, after all. Even if they tend to be "strong," sometimes, they don't yet have all their "ducks in a row." They still need us!

By keeping in mind what we've learned in this chapter, we can help our children find themselves while also helping them to become resilient and goal-oriented.

Everything above makes sense, but it is difficult to follow through given the tumultuous and hyper-fast age of new technology and digital media. You might think about how resilience can be fostered in such crucial times. Hence, you can ask, what is the importance of resilience in the digital age? Does technology make it easier or harder for children to cultivate resilience? In the following chapter, we'll explore answers to these biting questions.

CHAPTER 8

RESILIENCE IN THE DIGITAL AGE

"According to a 2021 study, almost half (42%) of 10-year-old children own their own smartphones. The older they are, the higher that percentage goes. The same study states that 71% of 12-year-olds and 91% of 14-year-olds have their own phone" (Gilchrist, 2022).

THE RELATIONSHIP BETWEEN RESILIENCE AND TECHNOLOGY IS an interesting one. While technology can benefit a child and help them build resilience, on the other hand, it comes with its own set of dangers. It has the strong potential to complement as well as negatively impact the process of resilience building in children.

The digital age is both a blessing and a curse. People are now more connected than ever before. With technology and the internet so easily accessible to kids, there is an equal risk of them falling into bad habits. Where technology provides them with immense opportunities for growth, it also puts them at risk of being spoiled by it.

How Are Children Affected by Growing up in a Digital Age?

> Growing up in the digital age has undoubtedly brought significant changes to the lives of children. The proliferation of technology and digital devices has opened up a world of opportunities and possibilities, but it has also presented unique challenges and impacts on the development and well-being of our children.

Today, it has become easier than ever to access information, and that too, not even by clicking a button but through a mere flick of a finger. This global access to information has revolutionized the globe and ways of understanding the world. We now know more about the people in other corners of the world. We can learn about anything anywhere in the world through the internet, which makes it beneficial.

On the downside, when I say anything is available, I mean anything is available. That means that even the inappropriate content is easily accessible. If you're not aware, horrendous things are available on the internet. As parents, we must be extra cautious about what our children can access, what they are watching, and whom they idealize. Even innocent-looking "cartoons" can be harmful these days, given that all different genres of cartoons are available over the internet. In such a situation, where it is inevitable to bar children from accessing the internet, it is incumbent upon parents to activate child locks and put age restrictions on the gadgets and devices that they are using. These precautions will help minimize the risk of being exposed to inappropriate content.

These days, kids are smarter than us when it comes to technology. Hence, it is advisable to monitor their online activity despite the placement of parental locks, as they can be easily surpassed through abundantly available proxies these days. Also, the parental locks are not 100 percent secure and reliable. This is not to scare you; instead, it is to help you understand the seriousness of the situation.

HOW SOCIAL MEDIA AFFECTS RESILIENCE

Social media is another significant influence of the digital era on our children. It has almost completely taken over the earth. When we were quarantined in our houses due to a global pandemic, it was the only tool of connection to the outer world. It allowed us to maintain some social contact. It was used to share hobbies, increase awareness, and other beneficial purposes.

However, social media has also been called "evil" for good reason. Those trends and pranks discussed previously are just the tip of the iceberg. Many children's lives now revolve around social media, and it's easy for them to become completely engrossed in it—sometimes to the point of obsession. It may emphasize how other people think of you, and how many "likes" you get defines your worth. Some people even have fake lives and personas online because they might feel that their real lives are mundane or lacking in attention, so social media offers a temporary escape into a more exciting or glamorous version of themselves. Their photographs may be AI-generated, manipulated, or otherwise altered to provide a misleading view of their lives or how they look. This breeds a terrible attitude of perfectionism in this generation. Our children are quick to compare themselves with unrealistic expectations set by people who probably don't even exist. When unrealistic expectations cannot be met, a deep depression can take hold of them. Maintaining a fake online persona can have serious repercussions, including various negative impacts on a child's mental health and general well-being, affecting their sense of identity, purpose, and resilience.

Unfortunately, some children will go to the opposite extreme because they believe they will never measure up. They lose hope and become helpless, and they stop trying or fighting. This can lead to isolation, anhedonia, and a lack of future ambitions, hopes, plans, or goals.

ADVANTAGES

It's not all bad. Despite its possible negative impacts, social media can also help children gain resilience by providing them with a social support system, particularly in instances where distance and restrictions may limit in-person connections, such as when COVID-19 initially appeared. However, these advantages are not only limited to a global epidemic for their occurrence. Social media, the internet, and all of our modern technologies can be used for empowerment and positivity when used with caution and understanding.

When used responsibly and in a balanced manner, social media can be a useful tool for kids who struggle with social anxiety. It might serve as a first step in making friends more easily and discovering a community that will encourage them so they will be inspired enough to "get out there."

Another example of where social media can benefit is if you undergo a massive relocation. We've spoken quite a bit about what a significant transition it is to move far away into a place they don't know. We've discussed how this can help them build resilience.

The potential benefits of social media in situations like relocation are huge. It's reassuring that your child can use social media to stay in touch with friends and family members who can't accompany them on a long-distance transfer across a continent, which is a substantial change for anyone.

This change contributes to their resilience since it functions as a form of support system.

If they have had a long day, everything was strange, the lunch lady was mean, and they tripped over a rock, at least they can come home and tell an online peer about it. Ideally, we would like to be the people they'd talk to. But realistically, kids need people their age to relate to as well, and social media provides that for them sometimes.

We'll need to encourage them to make new friends and cultivate new positive relationships, but they need not let go of the ones they already have. The ones they do have will likely offer comfort in times of uncertainty.

With the above in mind, you can see how social media and the internet can play a role in cultivating coping skills. For example, they can Google "ways to cope" with almost anything. It's that simple.

Let's take the scenario where you've moved to an entirely new place that's unfamiliar to you and has different cultures and/or languages. Social media and the internet can be helpful for a kid needing to research the local scene.

They could also try to follow people they meet on social media, thus making new friends. That's the thing these days: When people meet, they often find each other on Instagram or other social media platforms first.

Social media is a great way to spark conversation. For example, say your child meets a kid at school today and befriends them on social media. Later, they see said friend repost a quote about cats—they both like cats; just like that, conversation and a possible positive relationship spark.

In conclusion, social media can bring friends and communities together to contribute to a common good or offer mutual help. When people start trading their knowledge and compassion, it creates a healthy environment. It adds to the development of resilience while fostering the idea of requesting aid from others when needed. Social media has the potential to be a positive and influential tool.

DISADVANTAGES

While social media can offer opportunities for connection and information-sharing, it also challenges a child's ability to cultivate resilience. Parents, guardians, and educators must keep an eye on their children's online behavior, promote a healthy balance between online and offline interactions, and support kids in building a diverse set of social skills that they can use in a variety of contexts, such as critical thinking and digital literacy abilities.

One of the main concerns with social media is its impact on a child's self-esteem and mental well-being. As discussed before, it can lead to comparing themselves with others, which leaves them feeling like they are not good enough, which furthers insecurities kids already feel—especially teenagers going through puberty.

To a certain extent, the content a person connects with and publishes on social media can reveal their interests, values, beliefs, and personality. Teaching children to critically analyze the content they encounter and share on social media is a vital component of digital literacy and appropriate online behavior so they can identify that some "Miss pencil skirts and button-up shirts"—who share Barbara Streisand quotes—may not be as successful or elegant as they portray themselves to be.

These concerns can, unfortunately, include social media addiction. You may not believe it, but it's true. Even social media can be addictive. The dangers of this addiction are many, including using social media to distract them from shortcomings in their real lives, for example. This can lead to greater risks of depression and anxiety as well (Mayo Clinic Staff, 2022).

> "Social media addiction was not significantly correlated with resilience overall, although greater social media addiction was related to lower levels of determination" (Hurley, 2018).

When determination is scant, it can change their sense of purpose and ultimately diminish resilience in the face of obstacles. When you think about it, it makes sense that social media use or addiction causes insecurity and could harm one's development of resilience. It isn't easy to be resilient when everyone brings you down on the internet. It's also hard to remain resilient when everyone's "picture-perfect lives" are thrown in your face, and you're constantly reminded of your failures or shortcomings.

The same can be said for adults. It is a pit that is easily fallen into. We must demonstrate good social media usage by ensuring our eyes are not permanently glued to our phones. This way, we present a healthy balance, which can help our kids do the same. Comparing oneself to others and expressing discontent with one's appearance or circumstances can harm the person making the remarks and those who hear them. It is essential to promote open communication and a positive attitude. Promoting self-acceptance and teaching children to value their unique qualities can help them develop resilience, healthy relationships, and a positive self-image.

Another aspect to consider is the potential for social media to promote a passive consumption culture. Children may spend excessive time scrolling through their feeds, consuming content without engaging or participating. This passive consumption can hinder their abilities to develop essential life skills such as problem-solving, critical thinking, and interpersonal communication, which are all crucial for building resilience.

Passive consumption also deprives children of creativity and productivity. With time, it becomes hard for them to take initiative in any task because they are just used to receiving rather than producing. They lose their muscle memory of doing, creating, initiating, and completing any activity or task.

I haven't yet mentioned the physical risks that social media can have regarding safety. It's in the news, in the papers, online, and just about everywhere else: Human trafficking is not only a nightmare. It's real. Culprits very often watch their targets online. Human trafficking is not the only problem either. Individual predators often stalk the social media of their targets. It's a cruel world out there, and we need to be aware of that—even if it is uncomfortable to talk about. We must educate our children about privacy and safety on social media. Teaching children critical thinking and digital literacy skills will enable them to navigate the online world responsibly and make informed decisions about the content they interact with and post on social media. It also assists them in developing a positive and balanced connection with technology and digital communication. It also encourages them to focus on their strengths, talents, and uniqueness, which can lead to a more positive and healthier self-image.

How Digital Media and Entertainment Affect Resilience

For example, video games can enhance resilience and other skills, such as hand-eye coordination and problem-solving skills (Zaera, n.d.). Kids need to be able to think critically to solve a problem in a game. This is one of the positive impacts these games can have on them. It can also help relieve stress and unwind after a long day of studying.

Emotionally, it can be good because every time you don't get something right in a game, you typically become more determined to get it right the next time to get to that final "prize." See how that helps with building resilience?

When used to help relieve stress and unwind, it helps cultivate resilience because once you've rested and calmed down, you can return to the real world with a new view—ready to take on challenges again.

Online games are also an excellent creative outlet. There are many different types of games. It's not all guns and cars. There are artistic games, puzzle games, mind-stimulating games—almost anything you can think of.

A fun and stimulating game is a "visual novel game." These are stories you need to read, but animated characters are playing the scenes out. You then get to make choices for the characters, and different options lead to different outcomes. This is a prime example of how gaming, reading, and critical thinking can simultaneously happen.

Too Much of a Good Thing

Digital media, digital entertainment, and online content can significantly impact a child's development of resilience. While they can provide opportunities for learning, creativity, and social connections, excessive screen time, exposure to inappropriate content, and passive consumption can hinder resilience-building.

Some digital content, like video games or internet videos, can influence a child's emotional regulation and impulsive control. Some information may incite undesirable behavior, including violence. Excessive exposure to violent or inappropriate content might impair children's sensitivity to real-world issues and their ability to feel empathy and develop a sense of morality.

I'm not the person who would say, "Games or music made them do it." People still have the ability to make their own choices. However, when online content influences an impressionable kid to the extent of addiction, it can take their lives over.

Unfortunately, in our beautiful country, we've seen children try to "act out" their fantasies in school or elsewhere, which has led to unfortunate deaths. That's how serious it can be.

The following story is a fictional example to explain the point further but is based on true accounts of similar situations.

Gretha's childhood was marred by difficulties in her family and personal life. She was bullied at school because of her acne, and her parents had an unusually detached approach to parenting. Gretha, like many other young people in her situation, sought refuge in the virtual domain, seeking the comfort she couldn't find in the actual world. Her adventure began with simple online games, where her skill quickly allowed her to develop her own online community. This sphere introduced her to people worldwide, culminating in constructing a separate online identity.

Gretha could communicate via video and audio calls within this digital realm, but she preferred text-based chats with her camera turned off. She continued to utilize images of other people as her profile pictures. This virtual connection, however, gradually became an unhealthy fixation. Gretha's routine involved feigning attendance at school only to come home once her parents had departed for the day.

Her ploy was eventually exposed, resulting in stern reprimands for her absenteeism by her parents. As a result of facing the bullying at school and being unable to escape into her escapist online world as frequently, she fell into a deep melancholy. One day, a boy's callous behavior of knocking her meal from her hands and taunting her, elicited a dramatic reaction. Gretha, overcome by her fantasies, went for a pocketknife hidden in her school blazer and inflicted many wounds on the boy, who did not survive.

Just like that, a precious life was taken, and her life was ruined.

Similar situations have turned out far worse, and it's an incredibly scary thought when you have children who are online a lot. This won't happen to every child. However, we do need to ensure that a balance exists. Using parental controls, discussing the potential effects of media with children, and encouraging critical thinking skills can help children navigate the digital landscape in a healthier and more balanced manner.

> After many years, the above tragedy led to the naming of an official disorder: internet gaming disorder—though it still requires a significant amount of research (Nasution et al., 2019).
>
> It's when gaming takes over the life of someone so much that their physical life is negatively impacted.

Cyberbullying

Cyberbullying isn't a new concept. In fact, it has been around since the very moment that the internet became popular. Today, though, it's much more common to experience cyberbullying. One regrettable outcome of cyberbullying is suicide in teenagers and young people. It can truly get that bad. As parents, this is extremely worrying because we might not even know what is happening right under our noses.

Cyberbullying is a prominent worry in today's digital world, and it can have profound consequences for children's development and well-being. Because of its potential to inflict emotional discomfort, psychological suffering, and even long-term effects, it is a genuine ACE. You must assist your child in developing resilience in the face of this possible harm to their development and teach them the skills necessary to navigate through the problems posed by cyberbullying. This assistance can significantly improve their emotional and mental well-being and general growth.

Studies have shown that teens who have been victims of cyberbullying are more likely to experience social anxiety and "higher risks of other behavioral or emotional problems" (Calvete et al., 2022). The effects of cyberbullying can be deadly, but they can be combated by a good level of resilience and a growth mindset. This is crucial to prevent permanent psychological damage that could follow them throughout the rest of their lives. By developing resilience and a growth mentality, individuals can build the emotional tools needed to manage the obstacles of cyberbullying and overcome its harmful consequences.

A resilient child will not be as affected by cyberbullying, but that doesn't mean that it will not bother or affect them at all. It simply means they can face the conflict with their head held high.

Studies have also been conducted to show that there is an "intervention" method that may help. This is where you can involve the school. The specific study I am referring to is a study called Resilience ITP Intervention.

The main points are three phases. First, there's a self-affirmation phase. The second phase focuses on the statement that people can change (including online bullies). The third phase focuses on how individuals react to stressors that can also be changed (Calvete et al., 2022).

The result was generally positive, and to me it shows that education and further raising awareness does, in fact, make a much greater difference than we think it does. Bullies are people who are experiencing their own "demons" as well. Online bullies are no different, and if we can educate them and show them the damage they can inflict, then we might just be able to make a real difference.

One particular story that comes to my mind here, and I have obviously once again changed the names, is of a teenager I will call Mandy, who underwent significant cyberbullying. It was severe and relentless. Apart from being unable to escape to an online world, she was also bullied in real life. There was this older girl who seemed to just have it in for her.

In most schools, if you begin asking around, there will be one or two people who are known as the bullies of the school. There might even be a specific group, for that matter.

In Mandy's school, that was exactly the case. A group of girls picked on everyone, but the leader of the group targeted Mandy specifically for unknown reasons.

An educator had been watching the situation for some time and tried intervening when necessary. When he noticed that his small interventions didn't do much to help, he spoke to the older girl's parents and had them come in for a meeting.

He told the girl, "I'm not going to simply talk to you because talking to you hasn't helped. I'm a teacher, and you may not necessarily care what I think. Instead, I will show you the impact your actions can have."

There was an old television in the classroom—one of those old ones they rolled out on the trolley if the classroom had to watch an educational film. He pointed a dusty remote at the television, and it flickered on.

The short film that he chose to show her wasn't fictional. It was a documentary about a young boy who took his own life before the age of thirteen due to bullying. It was uncut, and it thoroughly discussed the pain that his family suffered and the guilt that the bullies would carry around for the rest of their lives.

That was a changing point for her; she apologized to Mandy and became an advocate for victims of bullying. This proves people can change, and educating them on the actual damage they can inflict is an excellent first step in helping them to do so.

It might sound somewhat superficial, but sometimes, the only thing that will break through the walls of a teenager is the cold, hard truth.

How Resilience Helps Victims of Cyberbullying

Resilience is critical in assisting victims of cyberbullying to cope with and overcome the negative consequences of such experiences. It allows victims to control their emotions in the face of cyberbullying. They are better equipped to deal with feelings of anger, fear, and melancholy, minimizing their overall well-being influence. It promotes a positive attitude, allowing victims to focus on their strengths and accomplishments rather than the negative parts of cyberbullying. Resilient individuals acquire efficient coping methods to deal with stress and hardship. They can direct their energy toward beneficial tasks. It allows individuals to face the adversity, learn from it, and thrive despite the unfavorable experiences. Building resilience gives people the emotional tools they need to recover their well-being and confidently navigate the digital world.

Victims of cyberbullying might not want to hear it, but the truth is even cyberbullying can be turned into a learning experience and an opportunity for growth. See it this way: These bullies are people with their own insecurities and psychological problems. If we can help our children understand that, then we might be able to lessen the blow for them. If they know where the bullying is coming from, it might just help them be more empathetic. That is an opportunity for emotional growth.

Many success stories worldwide also revolve around people who were bullied but stood up for themselves and worked harder than ever to prove everyone wrong. In the ideal world, there would be no bullying to begin with. There would be no need to prove anyone wrong about anything. Unfortunately, as you know, we do not live in the ideal world. But striving to prove others wrong shows determination and a sense of purpose. Do you see what I'm getting at?

When they are being bullied, these things won't necessarily be crystal clear to them. When you're really hurt, it doesn't matter what anyone says; it just hurts. Again, we need to validate those feelings and their adverse experiences. However, we can do that while still helping them to foster a sense of resilience.

WHAT YOU CAN DO TO HELP

Conversations are key. Have regular discussions about internet safety, the effects of cyberbullying, and their social circle. Most teenagers will not want to discuss these things with you; however, it's important to try and stimulate a conversation because they need to know that we're safe to talk to, and we need to recognize signs of bullying.

Cultivate offline resilience-building activities. Balance your child's digital experiences with offline activities that promote resilience. Encourage them to participate in sports, hobbies, or community activities that foster teamwork, problem-solving, and face-to-face interactions. Engaging in real-world experiences helps develop resilience in different contexts. A child may be academically resilient but suffer when faced with other challenges. They may be lost when a family tragedy or other difficult situation occurs. We want to help children develop true resilience in the face of all the challenges they'll experience, which entails exposing them to real-life settings where appropriate rather than "parrot-learning" reactions.

Monitor regularly. I believe that it is necessary for parents to inspect their children's phones randomly and regularly. This is not an invasion of privacy; this is supervision and responsible parenting. I also believe in transparency. My daughter knows I look through her phone and sometimes listen to her conversations. She knows that it is my job to monitor what she is doing. I don't hide it from her.

Establish internet rules. We can set some ground rules to help our kids in this technological age. These rules can be used for computers, cell phones, tablets, and other devices that can access the internet.

1. No using electronics during family dinners.
2. Set a time for when electronics need to be put away. (I recommend at least two hours before bedtime).
3. Keep device location switched off, and do not share photos where their whereabouts can be traced.
4. Parental locks should be added to Netflix, YouTube, and other apps where locks can be added.
5. The internet is not a necessity; it is a privilege. Kids should know that it can be taken away just as easily

as it can be given. This is not to threaten them but to teach them that if they break internet rules, it can be taken away.

6. Make up a list of certain websites that you know of that are not to be visited. Trust me, there are some sketchy websites out there. You need to be careful with this one because if we set out a list of websites, they might be curious enough to want to visit them just for the sake of it. Do a little research into how these websites can be permanently blocked.

7. For younger kids, screen time can be limited to weekends and only for a certain period of time. This can be done with older kids as well, but let's be real, they will use their phones during the week. Best to save yourself from the power struggle.

8. Parents are to have access to all electronics at all times.

9. No sharing personal contact information online.

10. No sharing or reposting of inappropriate photos or content.

11. No online bullying of any kind or taking part in pranks that could hurt others.

These are simple rules, and you can absolutely come up with your own. Your rules will depend on your child and your circumstances. Take some time to really think about it before setting up rules. Discuss it with your children, and make sure that they feel heard when concerns regarding the rules are brought to your attention. It's never a good thing to answer them in a dismissive way such as, "Because I said so." Explain your reasoning to them. You'd be surprised by how understanding kids can be when we actually talk to them.

In our next and final chapter, we will discuss our role in helping children build resilience—as either their parent, guardian, or teacher—in further detail. In the end, a lot of what their lives will be like one day comes down to us and how we make use of the important roles we've been given.

9

RESILIENT KIDS: OUR ROLE AS ADULTS

> The most significant determinant of resilience—noted in nearly every review or study of resilience in the last 50 years—is the quality of our close personal relationships, especially with parents and primary caregivers. Early attachments to parents play a crucial, lifelong role in human adaptation.
>
> —EILENE ZIMMERMAN

Let's talk about what may be considered the most essential part of fostering resilience in children: our roles as parents, guardians, and educators. Much of this chapter summarizes what we've discussed so far. The importance of our roles is too essential not to repeat. We're the ones who will be shaping their futures.

AS PARENTS OR GUARDIANS

Once again, we must be kids' number one source of support and comfort. While we remember the difference between insincere and genuine praise, we can encourage and support along the way. It's okay to be the parent who runs along the football field while cheering for the team. Blowing up balloons and getting a cake out is okay when they genuinely achieved something they're proud of. Make sure that they know that we really are proud of them.

We have the privilege and obligation of being an active parental figure and our children's primary support system. Prioritizing our presence and becoming more involved in their life can help them develop resilience and general well-being. Do not simply encourage kids to participate in activities. Show up and offer as much support as you can. It won't be possible to be present for every single practice, but the least we can do is make sure that we don't miss the big games and talk to them at night about their day, including what happened during practice.

We need to prioritize spending quality time with our children. Engage in meaningful conversations, participate in activities together, and show genuine interest in their lives. Being present and attentive will create a strong foundation of support.

We also need to be attuned to our children's emotions and provide them with emotional support, remembering to nurture their problem-solving skills by encouraging them to think critically and solve their challenges.

Be their advocate and champion. Support their interests and passions. Encourage them to pursue their goals and dreams. Celebrate their achievements—no matter how small—and provide reassurance and encouragement during setbacks. Let them know we believe in them and their ability to overcome obstacles.

A Recap of What Parents Should Do

- Empower your child with problem-solving techniques.
- Help your child understand and manage their emotions effectively.
- Help your child to be just as compassionate towards themselves as they are to others by encouraging kindness, self-care, and understanding towards themselves.
- Teach your child from a young age how important self-care is for their mental, physical, and emotional well-being.
- Be sure that your house is an inclusive and accepting environment where your child feels they belong and aren't an outsider.
- Encourage your child to think "glass half full" rather than "glass half empty."

- Encourage play and exploration.
- Encourage them to foster positive connections.
- Help them set up routines.
- Encourage healthy risk taking.
- Find support groups for kids with special needs.
- Ensure kids with diverse backgrounds have access to resources.
- Ensure that your child has a strong support system and knows when to ask for help.
- Foster critical thinking and problem-solving skills.
- Ensure that open and effective communication is present.
- Promote a growth mindset.
- Teach them about self-care.
- Encourage healthy coping skills.
- Foster autonomy and independence when possible.
- Support them while working through their identity and purpose.
- Encourage digital intelligence.
- Offer professional help to work through ACEs where necessary.
- Just *be there*.

> What we all need to remember is that we want our kids to develop resilience because of us, not despite us.

AS EDUCATORS

You might be here as both a parent and an educator, and it's helpful to know that you can help the kids in your classes and your own. Some of these suggestions resemble those made by parents. If you're not an educator, speak with one and offer advice like the ones listed below so everyone involved can have a collaborative and fruitful journey.

As a parent, you may have expectations for those who educate your children, and it is vital to discuss these with them. Teachers, like everyone else, are individuals who may or may not be aware of these facts about your kid. Maintain mutual respect in the discourse and cultivate positive connections with the teachers who work with your children.

What Educators Can Do

- Foster a supportive peer network by encouraging collaboration and teamwork in the classroom.
- Promote self-care and well-being by teaching students the importance of self-care, including stress management, healthy habits, and self-reflection.
- Continuously communicate and involve parents to maintain open and regular communication and have a collaborative approach in supporting students' resilience.

- Build strong teacher-student relationships to develop positive rapport with students based on trust, empathy, and understanding.
- Teach and model emotional intelligence to help students understand and manage their emotions by teaching them self-awareness, empathy, and effective communication skills.
- Foster problem-solving skills and create opportunities for students to develop their problem-solving abilities.
- Encourage resilience-building activities.
- Provide a balanced assessment approach and implement assessments that focus on growth, progress, and effort rather than just grades.
- Promote a growth mindset to encourage a belief that intelligence and abilities can be developed through effort and practice.
- Create a positive and inclusive classroom environment, creating a welcoming space where all students feel valued and respected.

Teachers can make or break a student's future. Let our kids reminisce about their school days fondly without carrying self-doubt around for their entire lives due to unsupportive educators.

MODELING RESILIENCE

One of the best and most effective ways adults can inspire resilience in children is by practicing resilience and actively modeling it. Children are more likely to develop a skill or trait if they are constantly exposed to it and see it in action.

We've touched on this before, which is a recap of the importance of setting a good example. As parents and educators, we are often their influencers, and kids are much more likely to follow us first. Parents and teachers are the first real outside influences kids are exposed to. They watch and learn from parents long before television and peer pressures arise.

The way your sweet three-year-old will try to walk in your shoes (literally), and your five-year-old will play with your makeup—smearing lipstick across their face, load blue eyeshadow on and around their eyes, or grab some tools and "fix" the television is exactly the way they'll be molded for the rest of their lives. It's never as plainly visible as when we observe the youngest little ones. They copy us because they look up to us; sometimes, that may not change over time. Other influences will enter the scene later, but we are the adults with whom they have the greatest contact. The other day, I heard about an eight-year-old who wanted her hair cut shoulder length just because her teacher had it cut that way. That means it's not just about the parents' influence; teachers play just as big of a role.

This influence stretches far beyond simply copying physical acts that we do or repeating what we say. That's why the saying, "Do what I say, and not what I do," is entirely out of line and impossible. You cannot tell your kids not to eat too many sweets if you've just finished a whole slab of chocolate by yourself.

Alright, maybe you can still eat the slab—just not where they can see it. All jokes aside, if we want kids to act in certain ways, we must first commit to behaving ourselves.

It goes as deep as emotional intelligence, respectful behavior, and resilience.

> "'You're on a plane, there's turbulence—you don't look at the guy next to you who's hysterical,' Dr. Ginsburg said. 'You look at the flight attendants, to see if they're still serving snack mix'" (Vance, 2021).

This quote makes a great point and is precisely why we must model emotional control and resilience. We're the ones they will look to for expertise and answers when the "grapes" really hit the fan. We're the flight attendants who must keep calm and smile gently when the turbulence hits.

And trust me, just like lemons, the grapes will hit the fan several times.

YOU FIRST

Now that you understand your role as support systems, sources of stability, and resilience models for your kids, you know that we need to take care of ourselves first to take care of our kids. We've already discussed the importance of self-care, so let's go over it again. Modeling self-care is critical since self-care is another part of resilience building.

Think about it this way:

On a flight, when the flight attendants explain how to use oxygen masks, they always emphasize that we need to put on our own masks first before we turn to help children or the elderly. To some, it may sound selfish, but it isn't. How can you help them if your oxygen runs out? Who will help them if you succumb to whatever negative incident befalls you?

It's exactly the same concept here. Who will look after your children if you're not healthy enough physically or mentally to do so? It would be best if you were in good health to ensure that you can help them be the best they can be.

Our mental health is especially important when it comes to our kids because it will affect how we behave in certain situations. If we take care of it, we can be sure that our actions and reactions will be more carefully calculated.

To look after our mental health, we can do the following:

- Take breaks when we need them. It's okay to rest even if we're fighting to be resilient. We're still human.

- Make use of the support systems that we have, and if we don't have a solid support system in place, build one by connecting with people who have similar interests.
- Seek the help of professionals if we need it.
- Indulge in healthy practices such as getting enough sleep and healthy eating. And don't forget the exercise!
- Don't blame ourselves for bad things that happen. Those "lemons" don't pick who they're thrown at; they're just thrown randomly.
- Admit when we need help and seek out a support system beyond professionals—family, friends, coworkers.
- Work for our own happiness and fulfillment as well. We are parents, but before we were parents, we were people. It doesn't matter how much time goes by; we'll always be those people.

There's a lot more to it than that, and a lot more that you can do, but this is a good place to start. You're a parent, but you're a human being first. Before you can be the best parent that you can be, you need to be kind to yourself. Kindness towards ourselves is one of the best examples we can set for our children. It will enhance their self-esteem—as well as our own—and their confidence as well.

One thing that you need to remember as you carry on with the wild ride that is parenting: You are enough, and you have what it takes to be a good parent as long as you try your best.

HELPING A WHOLE GENERATION

It's amazing how much impact we can have when we work together, and I'd like to ask you to take a moment to help me support other parents as they navigate their way along this challenging yet rewarding path.

Simply by sharing your honest opinion of this book and a little about your own parenting journey, you'll show new readers exactly where they can find the guidance they're looking for.

WANT TO HELP OTHERS?

Thank you so much for your support. The next generation needs us, and I'm so grateful to have you on board.

To leave a review scan the QR Code.

CONCLUSION

The key points that you can take away from this book are as follow:

- You are the first order of business, and you need to take care of yourself first.
- Remember what resilience is and what it is not.
- Know why being resilient matters.
- Children can be resilient regardless of their background or whether they may have more unique circumstances.
- A growth mindset is important. Know how to foster that.
- Understand the importance of problem-solving skills.
- Recognize how important it is that we need to be present and involved in their lives.
- Know how the digital age affects our kids and their resilience both positively and negatively.
- Understand our roles as parents and even educators.

There is no such thing as "too late." Yes, cultivating resilience from a young age has many benefits, but it is never too late to change your life and your child's life. It's always possible to start being the person you want to see them grow into. It's always possible to try.

After having journeyed through resilience, its importance, psycho-social issues, and the role of parents in these trying times of digitization, we are finally at the end. We have learned how to make our children able to survive tragedies, adapt to change, discover their purpose, and, above all, succeed and grow.

Those who have come this far are now more equipped to assist their children. It shows that you, as a parent or guardian, are really invested in your child's well-being and will practice what you have learned from this book.

I have shared with you the accumulation of my lifelong learning as a psychiatrist and a mother. There were times when there seemed to be no light at the end of the tunnel when nothing made sense. But eventually, with the proper support, I came out and made the world possible for myself and my daughter. She is now my shining star; she is my pride.

As parents, we are tasked with one heck of a responsibility, and sometimes, it feels overwhelming to know that the person you are raising may raise other people, who may raise other people, and so on. What you teach them now will impact future generations to come. It can seem daunting, but it can turn out well if you remain resilient.

Many of you who might find yourself in that dark tunnel should remember that there is a light on the other side. To all the struggling parents, I can relate to your daily concerns;

I wrote this book for you. I hope this generation and those that follow are resilient and capable of creating a better tomorrow. I hope that by sharing my story and knowledge with you, I can play a small part in shaping the future of our beautiful and diverse world. In the end, if combined, the right amount of support, resilience, not giving up, and tons of courage are a recipe to stand through any situation in life. And make lemonade of every lemon that life tosses to you!

We can ensure that this generation and those who follow are resilient and capable of creating a better tomorrow. It takes some hard work now, but the result will surely be worth it. I hope that by sharing my story and my knowledge with you, I get to play a small part in the future of our beautiful, diverse world.

You've made it to the end of this book. Now go and make a difference.

You are ready!

REFERENCES

ACES and toxic stress: Frequently asked questions. (n.d.). Center on the Developing Child at Harvard University. https://developingchild. harvard.edu/resources/aces-and-toxic-stress-frequently-asked-questions/

Acknowledging your child's feelings will lead to resilient kids. (n.d.). Child & Adolescent Behavioral Health. https://www.childandadolescent. org/raising-children-who-are-resilient/

American Academy of Pediatrics. (n.d.). *How safe, stable relationships can prevent toxic stress in children.* Healthychildren.org. https://www. healthychildren.org/English/news/Pages/Safe-Stable-Relationship s-Prevent-Toxic-Stress.aspx

Anilc, R. (2018, June 7). *7 signs of a resilient child and how to help your child.* Parentcircle.com. https://www.parentcircle.com/signs-of-a-resilient-child/article

Are there mental health benefits of video games? (n.d.). WebMD. https:// www.webmd.com/mental-health/mental-health-benefits-of-vide o-games#091e9c5e8215d022-1-2

Bellis, M. A., Hughes, K., Ford, K., Hardcastle, K. A., Sharp, C. A., Wood, S., Homolova, L., & Davies, A. (2018). Adverse child-hood experiences and sources of childhood resilience: A retrospective study of their combined relationships with child health and educational attendance. *BMC Public Health, 18(1)*. https://doi. org/10.1186/s12889-018-5699-8

Benefits of problem-solving in the K-12 classroom. (2022, October 5). Institute of Competition Sciences. . https://www.competitionsciences. org/2022/10/05/benefits-of-problem-solving-in-the-k-12-classroom/

Building resilience in children. (2014, September 4). Healthychildren.org. https://www.healthychildren.org/English/healthy-living/emotio nal-wellness/Building-Resilience/Pages/Building-Resilience-in-Children.aspx

Building resilience, fostering identity. (2015, November 11). UW College of Education. https://education.uw.edu/news/building-resilienc e-fostering-identity

Building your resilience with self-care. (2020, May 12). TELUS Health. https://lifeworks.com/en/resource/building-your-resilience-self-care

Calvete, E., Orue, I., Nerea Cortazar, A. E., & Fernández-González, L. (2022). A growth mindset intervention to promote resilience against online peer victimization: A randomized controlled trial. *Computers in Human Behavior, 135*. https://doi.org/10.1016/j.chb.2022.107373

Cauberghe, V., De Jans, S., Hudders, L., & Vanwesenbeeck, I. (2021, October 16). Children's resilience during Covid-19 confinement. A child's perspective–Which general and media coping strategies are useful? *Journal of Community Psychology*. https://doi.org/10.1002/jcop.22729

CBT Professionals. (2013, December 14). *The 7 C's of resilience*. CBT Professionals. https://cbtprofessionals.com.au/the-7-cs-of-resilience/

Center City Pediatrics. (2018, September 11). *Praise your child's failures. Yes, their failures*. Center City Pediatrics. https://centercitypedia trics.com/praise-failure-growth-mindset-kids/

CEO Views Magazine. (2019, October 10). *It is hard to fail, but it is worse never to have tried to succeed." –Theodore Roosevelt.* Medium. https://medium.com/@cioviewssocial/it-is-hard-to-fail-but-it-is-worse-never-to-have-tried-to-succeed-theodore-roosevelt-a2c264e3f525

Chatterjee, R. (2019, January 5). *Six ways to raise a resilient child.* The Guardian. https://www.theguardian.com/lifeandstyle/2019/jan/05/six-ways-to-raise-a-resilient-child

Cherry, K. (2022, October 6). *10 ways to improve your resilience.* Verywellmind.com. https://www.verywellmind.com/ways-to-become-more-resilient-2795063

Cherry, K. (2023, March 15). *What is resilience?* Verywellmind.com. https://www.verywellmind.com/characteristics-of-resilience-2795062#toc-examples-of-resilience

Childhood resilience. (2021, November 22). Substance Abuse and Mental Health Services Association. https://www.samhsa.gov/homelessness-programs-resources/hpr-resources/childhood-resilience

Children and technology: Parent guidelines for every age. (2017, June 29). IEEE Technology and Society. https://technologyandsociety.org/children-and-technology-guidelines-for-parents-rules-for-every-age/

Chowbey, P. & Barley, R. (2022, February 18). Building resilience: young children from minority ethnic backgrounds starting school in a multi-ethnic society. *British Journal of Sociology of Education, 42 (3)* 1–18. https://doi.org/10.1080/01425692.2022.2030672

Collier, E. (2020, May 6). *The importance of routine for children: Free weekly planner.* High Speed Training. https://www.highspeedtraining.co.uk/hub/the-importance-of-routine-for-children/

Cuppy, C. (2021, June 17). *4 steps to teaching your child emotional control.* Focus on the Family. https://www.focusonthefamily.com/parentin g/4-steps-to-teaching-your-child-emotional-control/

Curletto, A. (n.d.). *Developing a sense of purpose in youth.* James Stanfield Co. https://stanfield.com/developing-a-sense-of-purpose-in-youth/

Darling-Hammond, L. (1998, March 1). *Unequal opportunity: race and education.* The Brookings Institution. https://www.brookings.edu/ articles/unequal-opportunity-race-and-education/

De Almientoz Santos, Z. & Soares, A. B. (n.d.). Social skills, coping, resilience and problem-solving in psychology university students. *Liberabit, 24(1),* 131–145. https://www.redalyc.org/ journal/686/68656777009/html/

Degges-White, S. (2021, October 15). *Personal and social identity: Who are you through others' eyes.* Psychology Today. https://www.psychol-ogytoday.com/intl/blog/lifetime-connections/202110/personal-an d-social-identity-who-are-you-through-others-eyes

Dewar, G. (2017, July 2). *The authoritative parenting style: An evidence-based guide.* Parenting Science. https://parentingscience.com/authoritative-parenting-style/

DiMaria, L. (2022, April 25). *The importance of a child's social identity.* Verywellmind.com https://www.verywellmind.com/the-importanc e-of-a-childs-social-identity-1066758

Dowshen, S. (2020, April). *Childhood stress: How parents can help.* KidsHealth. https://kidshealth.org/en/parents/stress.html

Duany, E. (2022, June 1). *Character traits of resilient children: 7 main characteristics.* Drduany.com. https://drduany.org/character-traits-resilien t-children/

Early years learning framework (n.d.). Kindalin. https://www.kindalin. com.au/eylf/1-0-children-have-a-strong-sense-of-identity/

Educating 21ˢᵗ century children: Emotional well-being in the digital age. (n.d.). OECD iLibrary. https://www.oecd-ilibrary.org/sites/2d4352c2-en/ index.html?itemId=/content/component/2d4352c2-en

Eisenburg, D.B. (2020, April 23). *Resilience is independence: Kids who think "I Can Do This" turn challenges into growth.* Connecticut Children's. https://www.connecticutchildrens.org/coronavirus/ resilience-is-independence-kids-who-think-i-can-do-this-turn -challenges-into-growth/

Erieau, C. (2019, February 20). *The 50 best resilience quotes.* Driven. https:// home.hellodriven.com/articles/the-50-best-resilience-quotes/

Firestone, L. (2011, December 6). *How to bully-proof your children by building their resilience.* Psychology Today https://www.psycholo-gytoday.com/intl/blog/compassion-matters/201112/how-bully-proo f-your-children-building-their-resilience

Flanagan, L. (2017, May 18). *How parents can help kids develop a sense of purpose.* KQED. https://www.kqed.org/mindshift/48013/how-parents-can-help-kids-develop-a-sense-of-purpose

Frydenberg, E., Deans, J., & Liang, R. (2021, June 25). Developing coping skills in the early years: A positive educational approach. *The Palgrave Handbook of Positive Education*, 369–393. https://doi. org/10.1007/978-3-030-64537-3_15

Geall, L. (n.d.). *Could this simple shift in attitude be the key to feeling more resilient in these wild times?* Stylist. https://www.stylist.co.uk/health/ mental-health/growth-mindset-benefits-resilience/448518

Gilchrist, K. (2022, November 25). *Don't want to give your kid a smartphone? Here are some alternatives.* CNBC. https://www.cnbc.com/2022/11/25/how-to-know-when-to-give-a-child-a-smartphone-what-are-the-alternatives.html

Ginsburg, K. (2019, May 29). *Building resilience: The 7 Cs.* Center for Parent and Teen Communication. https://parentandteen.com/building-resilience-in-teens/

Gonser, S. (2021, March 26). *5 Ways to build resilience in students.* Edutopia. https://www.edutopia.org/article/5-ways-build-resilience-students/

Gordon, S. (2022, July 22). *Warning signs your child is being bullied at school.* Verywellfamily.com. https://www.verywellfamily.com/signs-of-bullying-621041

Gordon, S. (2022, July 22). *What are the effects of cyberbullying?* Verywellfamily.com. https://www.verywellfamily.com/what-are-the-effects-of-cyberbullying-460558

Great leaders have emotional control. (n.d.). SIGMA Assessment Systems. https://www.sigmaassessmentsystems.com/emotional-control/

GreatSchools Staff. (2022, March 2). *How to help a child find their purpose.* Greatschools.org. https://www.greatschools.org/gk/articles/how-to-help-a-child-find-their-purpose/

Gross-Loh, C. (2016, December 16). *How praise became a consolation prize.* The Atlantic. https://www.theatlantic.com/education/archive/2016/12/how-praise-became-a-consolation-prize/510845/

Growing up resilient: Ways to build resilience in children and youth. (n.d.). CAMH. https://www.camh.ca/en/health-info/guides-and-publications/growing-up-resilient

Growth mindset: 3 reasons you struggle to teach it. (n.d.). Big Life Journal. https://biglifejournal.com/blogs/blog/obstacles-teaching-kids-growth-mindset

Hart, A., Heaver, B., Brunnberg, E., Sandberg, A., MacPherson, H., Coombe, S., & Kourkoutas, E. (2016). Resilience-building with disabled children and young people: A review and critique of the academic evidence base. *International Journal of Child, Youth and Family Studies, 5(3)*, 394. https://www.academia.edu/73876232/Resilience_Building_with_Disabled_Children_and_Young_People_A_Review_and_Critique_of_the_Academic_Evidence_Base

Healy, M. (2014, June 10) *The resilient child.* Psychology Today. https://www.psychologytoday.com/intl/blog/creative-development/201407/the-resilient-child

Helping children develop a positive identity. (2022, February 3). Holt International. https://www.holtinternational.org/helping-children-develop-a-positive-identity/

Helping children learn how to manage emotions. (2018, March 5). Psych Central. https://psychcentral.com/blog/helping-children-learn-how-to-manage-emotions#1

Helping your child to have a strong sense of identity. (n.d.). Department of Education and Early Childhood Development. https://www.patterson-lakes-ps.vic.edu.au/uploaded_files/media/2.helping_your_child_to_have_a_strong_sense_of_identity_.pdf

Herzog, J. I. & Schmahl, C. (2018). Adverse childhood experiences and the consequences on neurobiological, psychosocial, and somatic conditions across the lifespan. *Frontiers in Psychiatry, 9(420).* https://doi.org/10.3389/fpsyt.2018.00420

Hook, B. *Can digital technology improve resilience?* (2020, September 2). Resilience Institute. https://resiliencei.com/blog/digital-technolog y-improve-resilience

How does social media use impact on wellbeing? (n.d.). Educare. https:// www.educare.co.uk/news/how-does-social-media-use-impac t-on-wellbeing

How to help your Black child develop resilience in the face of racism and discrimination. (n.d.). Texas Children's Hospital. https://www.tex aschildrens.org/blog/how-help-your-black-child-develop-resilien ce-face-racism-and-discrimination

How to talk to your children about bullying. (n.d.). Unicef. https://www. unicef.org/end-violence/how-talk-your-children-about-bullying

How you can help your children build resilience against common social media concerns. (2018, January 5). HuffPost. https://www.huffingtonpost.co.uk/ entry/parents-need-to-know-helping-their-children-navigate-c ommon-social-media-problems_uk_5a4cdf28e4b06d1621bc3063

Hurewitz, S. (2022, March 11). *Study reveals how parents may help children develop resilience in the face of a public health crisis.* Duke Center for Child & Family Policy. https://childandfamilypolicy.duke. edu/news/study-reveals-how-parents-can-play-a-key-role-in-hel ping-their-children-develop-resilience-in-the-face-of-a-public-hea lth-crisis/

Hurley, K. (2020, November 24). *How to build resilience in children: Strategies to strengthen your kids.* Psycom.net. https://www.psycom. net/build-resilience-children

Hurley, K. (2022, July 14). *What is resilience? Your guide to facing life's challenges, adversities, and crises.* Everyday Health. https://www.ev erydayhealth.com/wellness/resilience/

Hurley, L.N. (2018). *The relationship between resilience, coping, and social media.* Eastern Illinois University. https://thekeep.eiu.edu/cgi/viewcontent.cgi?article=4680&context=theses

Jacobson, H. and Bregman, P. (2021, September 24). *The 2 biggest mental traps that hold us back from becoming more resilient and confident in life.* CNBC. https://www.cnbc.com/2021/09/24/how-to-overcome-mental-traps-that-destroy-our-confidence.html

Jeremy. (2019, July 31). *Encouraging healthy risk-taking.* TeamKids. https://www.teamkids.com.au/encouraging-healthy-risk-taking/

Jon. (2022, February 1). *Resilience vs resistance: What's the difference?* Think Positive. https://thinkpositivecheck.com/resilience-vs-resistance-whats-the-difference/

Jones, C. M., Scholes, L., Johnson, D., Katsikitis, M., & Carras, M. C. (2014). Gaming well: Links between videogames and flourishing mental health. *Frontiers in Psychology, 5(260)*, 1–8. https://doi.org/10.3389/fpsyg.2014.00260

Just how harmful is social media? Our experts weigh-in. (2021, September 27). Columbia University Irving Medical Center. https://www.publichealth.columbia.edu/news/just-how-harmful-social-media-our-experts-weigh

Kagan, J. (2019). *What is a special needs child?* Investopedia. https://www.investopedia.com/terms/s/specialneedschild.asp

Keith, K.L. (2022, May 29). *5 easy steps to a daily family schedule.* Verywellfamily.com https://www.verywellfamily.com/easy-steps-to-a-daily-family-schedule-620635

KidsHealth Behavioral Health Experts. (2018). *Dealing with addiction.* Kidshealth.org. https://kidshealth.org/en/teens/addictions.html

LaBianca J. (2022, December 2). *10 silent signs your child is being bullied.* Reader's Digest. https://www.rd.com/list/bullying-signs/

Langevin, M. (2020, October 13). *Using growth mindset to get over your fear of failure.* Mind Cafe. https://medium.com/mind-cafe/using-growth-mindset-to-get-over-your-fear-of-failure-3e1ecc71f8bf

Learning resilience through identity. (2021, October 19). Bright Kids Early Learning Centre. https://brightkidscentre.com.au/learning-resilience-through-identity/

Leaticiakaggwa@lifespeak.com. (2018, October 16). *How playing games can improve your resilience.* Thrive Global. https://community.thrive-global.com/how-playing-games-can-improve-your-resilience/

Lee, E.H. (2022, February 24). *Resilience: 5 ways to help children and teens learn it.* Harvard Health Publishing. https://www.health.harvard.edu/blog/resilience-5-ways-to-help-children-and-teens-learn-it-202202242694

Linnell-Olson, L. (2021, May 2). *Teaching your child to have a growth mindset.* Verywellfamily.com https://www.verywellfamily.com/tips-for-teaching-your-child-to-have-a-growth-mindset-4014842#toc-1-teach-your-children-its-okay-to-be-wrong

Lockhart, A.T. (2020, August 3). *5 characteristics of highly resilient kids, according to a pediatric psychologist.* PureWow. https://www.purewow.com/family/characteristics-of-resilient-kids

Lonczak, H.S. (2019, February 19). *How to build resilience in children: 30+ tips & examples.* Positive Psychology. https://positivepsychology.com/resilience-in-children/#resilient-kids

Macedo, T., Wilheim, L., Gonçalves, R., Coutinho, E. S. F., Vilete, L., Figueira, I., & Ventura, P. (2014). Building resilience for future adversity: a systematic review of interventions in non-clinical samples of adults. *BMC Psychiatry, 14(1).* https://doi.org/10.1186/s12888-014-0227-6

Malin, H. (2019, January 31). *Teaching purpose for resilience and flourishing.* Harvard Education Publishing Group. https://www.hepg.org/blog/teaching-purpose-for-resilience-and-flourishing

Marano, H. E. (2003, May 1). *The art of resilience.* Psychology Today. https://www.psychologytoday.com/us/articles/200305/the-art-resilience

Markel, A. (2023, January 24). *4 simple self-care rituals to help you build more resilience.* Entrepreneur. https://www.entrepreneur.com/living/4-simple-self-care-rituals-to-help-you-build-more-resilience/442344

Markham, L. (2023, February 15). *Resilient kids have parents who do these 10 things.* Motherly. https://www.mother.ly/parenting/how-to-raise-kids-resilience/

Marrott, K. (2017, July 17). *Resistance vs. resilience: 5 resiliency techniques to cope with accelerating change.* Intermountain Health. https://intermountainhealthcare.org/blogs/topics/transforming-healthcare/2017/07/resistance-vs-resilience/

Mayo Clinic Staff. (2020, October 27). *How to build resiliency.* Mayo Clinic. https://www.mayoclinic.org/tests-procedures/resilience-training/in-depth/resilience/art-20046311

Mayo Clinic Staff. (2022, February 26). *Teens and social media use: What's the impact?* Mayo Clinic. https://www.mayoclinic.org/healthy-lifestyle/tween-and-teen-health/in-depth/teens-and-social-media-use/art-20474437

Melbourne Child Psychology & School Psychology Services. (n.d.) *How and why kids need to learn resilience.* (n.d.). Melbourne Child

Psychology. https://www.melbournechildpsychology.com.au/blog/
how-and-why-kids-need-to-learn-resilience/

Millacci, T.S. (2021, December 29). *How to nurture a growth mindset in
kids: 8 best activities*. Positive Psychology. https://positivepsychology.
com/growth-mindset-for-kids/

Morin, A. (2020, August 31). *Coping strategies for kids*. Verywellfamily.com.
https://www.verywellfamily.com/coping-skills-for-kids-4586871

Morin, A. (2020, May 29). *Sample list of rules for your teen's electronics*.
Verywellfamily.com. https://www.verywellfamily.com/sample-cel
l-phone-tv-computer-rules-for-teenagers-1094878

Morin, A. (2021, April 13). *Teach kids how to solve their own problems and
make good decisions*. Verywellfamily.com. https://www.verywellfam-
ily.com/teach-kids-problem-solving-skills-1095015

Morin, A. (2021, April 25). *How to help overly emotional kids deal with their
big feelings*. Verywellfamily.com. https://www.verywellfamily.com/
how-to-help-an-overly-emotional-child-4157594

Murphy, A. (2019, October 17). *30 growth mindset quotes to change your life*.
Declutter the Mind. https://declutterthemind.com/blog/growth-
mindset-quotes/

Nahata, K. (2020, August 5). *How to promote resilience in special needs children amid Covid 19?* Starlit Ability Enhancement Services. https://
www.starlitservices.com/how-to-promote-resilience-in-special-nee
ds-children-amid-covid-19/

Nasution, F. A., Effendy, E., & Amin, M. M. (2019). Internet gaming disorder (IGD): A case report of social anxiety. *Macedonian
Journal of Medical Sciences, 7(16)*, 2664–2666. https://doi.org/10.3889/
oamjms.2019.398

NDFAuthors. (2023, April 5). *The benefits of art and creativity in early childhood education*. The Early Years Blog by Novak Djokovic Foundation. https://novakdjokovicfoundation.org/the-benefits-of-art-and-creativity-in-early-childhood-education/

Nelson, C. A., Bhutta, Z. A., Burke Harris, N., Danese, A., & Samara, M. (2020). Adversity in childhood is linked to mental and physical health throughout life. *BMJ, 371(371)*. https://doi.org/10.1136/bmj.m3048

Newman, L., & Leggett, N. (2019, November 2021). *Five ways parents can help their kids take risks – and why it's good for them*. The Conversation. https://theconversation.com/five-ways-parents-can-help-their-kids-take-risks-and-why-its-good-for-them-120576

Novoa, C. (2020, August 27). *Adversity in early childhood*. Center for American Progress. https://www.americanprogress.org/article/adversity-early-childhood/

Nurturing resilience in a world of racial aggression and violence. (n.d.). Embrace Race. https://www.embracerace.org/resources/talking-race-kids-nurturing-resilience-in-a-world-of-racial-aggression-and-violence

Papakonstantinopoulou, A., Spinthourakis, J., & Dimakos, I. (n.d.). *Empowering children's identity through a resilience framework*. Children's Identity and Citizenship. http://www.cicea.eu/pdfs/2019CONF/75_PAPAKONSTANTINOPOULOU_SPINTOURAKIS_DIMAKOS_SPYRALATOS_Empowering-childrens-identity-through-a-resilience-framework.pdf

Parker, J. & Folkman, J. (2015). Building resilience in students at the intersection of special education and foster care challenges, strategies, and resources for educators. *Building Resilience in Students at the Intersection of Special Education and Foster Care, 24(2)*. https://files.eric.ed.gov/fulltext/EJ1090358.pdf

Paulynice, J. (2020, September 22). *How to instill a sense of purpose in kids.* Medium. https://medium.com/@paulynice/how-to-instill-a-sense-o f-purpose-in-kids-2ae3b1166732

Pells, R. (2017, June 30). *Moderate use of social media 'builds resilience and wellbeing in young people', report suggests.* The Independent. https://www.independent.co.uk/news/education/education-news/ social-media-wellbeing-young-people-moderate-use-report-epi-f acebook-twitter-a7815316.html

Perry, C. (2022, December 20). *Authoritative parenting: The pros and cons, according to a child psychologist.* Parents.com. https://www. parents.com/parenting/better-parenting/style/authoritativ e-parenting-the-pros-and-cons-according-to-a-child-psycholo- gist/#:~:text=Resiliency

Persistence and resilience: Empowered for success. (2021, July 21). Jay Wren. https://www.jaywren.com/persistence-and-resilience/

Pillow, D. R., Malone, G. P., & Hale, W. J. (2015). The need to belong and its association with fully satisfying relationships: A tale of two measures. *Personality and Individual Differences, 74,* 259–264. https:// doi.org/10.1016/j.paid.2014.10.031

Pinola, M. (2019). *How and when to limit kids' tech use.* The New York Times. https://www.nytimes.com/guides/smarterliving/family-technology

Problem-solving skills—enhancing children's resilience. (n.d.). Canadian Child Care Federation. https://cccf-fcsge.ca/wp-content/up- loads/2020/05/RS_90-e.pdf

Raising happy kids: Building resilience in children. (2021, November 4). Bright Horizons. https://www.brighthorizons.com/resources/ Article/making-happy-happen-building-resilience-in-children

Raypole, C. (2020, April 28). *How to control your emotions: 11 strategies to try.* Healthline. https://www.healthline.com/health/how-to-control-your-emotions

Recognizing and treating child traumatic stress. (2023, June 28). Substance Abuse and Mental Health Services Administration. https://www.samhsa.gov/child-trauma/recognizing-and-treating-child-traumatic-stress

Reflecting on social justice foundational concepts. (n.d.). Libraries Teaching and Learning. https://lo.library.wisc.edu/DEI_foundations/lesson_1.html

Relationships and child development. (2023, March 22). Raising Children Network. https://raisingchildren.net.au/newborns/development/understanding-development/relationships-development

Resilience guide for parents and teachers. (2012). American Psychological Association. https://www.apa.org/topics/resilience/guide-parents-teachers

Resilience in autistic children and teenagers. (n.d.). Raising Children Network. https://raisingchildren.net.au/autism/development/social-emotional-development/resilience-autistic-children-teenagers

Resilience, stress and a growth mindset. (n.d.). Scotland Deanery. https://www.scotlanddeanery.nhs.scot/trainee-information/thriving-in-medicine/resilience-stress-and-a-growth-mindset/

Resilience. (n.d.). Center on the Developing Child at Harvard University. https://developingchild.harvard.edu/science/key-concepts/resilience/

Resilience: how to build it in children 3-8 years. (2021, April 20). Raising Children Network. https://raisingchildren.net.au/school-age/behaviour/understanding-behaviour/resilience-how-to-build-it-in-children-3-8-years

Riopel, L. (2019, January 20). *Resilience examples: what key skills make you resilient?* PositivePsychology.com. https://positivepsychology.com/resilience-skills/#characteristics-resilient-person

Riopel, L. (2019, September 3). *The Connor Davidson + brief resilience scales.* PositivePsychology.com. https://positivepsychology.com/connor-davidson-brief-resilience-scale/#:~:text=References-

Robins, R. (2023, March 8). *Clinical psychologist: Social media harming youth mental health.* Govtech.com https://www.govtech.com/education/k-12/clinical-psychologist-social-media-harming-youth-mental-health

Robson, D. (2022, November 9). *How to avoid bad choices.* BBC. https://www.bbc.com/future/article/20221101-how-to-teach-kids-to-make-great-choices

Ronen, T. (2021). The role of coping skills for developing resilience among children and adolescents. *The Palgrave Handbook of Positive Education,* 345–368. https://doi.org/10.1007/978-3-030-64537-3_14

Samis, M. (2010, February 20). *Creating routines for love and learning.* ZERO to THREE. https://www.zerotothree.org/resource/creating-routines-for-love-and-learning/

Sanders, J., Munford, R., & Liebenberg, L. (2016). The role of teachers in building resilience of at risk youth. *International Journal of Educational Research, 80,* 111–123. https://doi.org/10.1016/j.ijer.2016.10.002

Sandstrom, H., & Huerta, S. (2013). *The negative effects of instability on child development: A research synthesis low-income working families.* Urban Institute. https://www.urban.org/sites/default/files/publication/32706/412899-The-Negative-Effects-of-Instability-on-Child-Development-A-Research-Synthesis.PDF

Sanvictores, T. & Mendez, M. D. (2022, September 18). Types of parenting styles and effects on children. National Library of Medicine. https://www.ncbi.nlm.nih.gov/books/NBK568743/#:~:text=This%20 article

Sashin, D. (2020, April 2). *Helping children turn failures into success through growth mindset.* Stanford Medicine. https://scope-blog.stanford.edu/2020/04/02/helping-children-turn-failures-into-success-through-growth-mindset/

Scher, J. (2013, August 30). *Resilience and perseverance in this time of change.* WhatTheyThink. https://whattheythink.com/articles/65 015-resilience-perseverance-time-change/

Schipani, D. 5 *reasons to establish a toddler routine.* (2022, December 29). Parents.com. https://www.parents.com/toddlers-preschoolers/ development/social/establishing-toddler-routines/

Signs your child is being bullied—tip sheet. (n.d.). Stomp Out Bullying. https://www.stompoutbullying.org/tip-sheet-signs-your-child-bein g-bullied

6 essential coping skills for children. (2021, December 22). Lumiere Children's Therapy. https://www.lumierechild.com/lumiere-childrens-therap y/6-coping-skills-for-children

Smith, J. (2020, September 25). *Growth vs fixed mindset: How what you think affects what you achieve.* Mindset Health. https://www.mindset-health.com/matter/growth-vs-fixed-mindset

Southwick, S. M., Sippel, L., Krystal, J., Charney, D., Mayes, L., & Pietrzak, R. (2016). Why are some individuals more resilient than others: the role of social support. *World Psychiatry, 15(1),* 77–79. https://doi.org/10.1002/wps.20282

Staake, J. (2023, January 27). *20 growth mindset activities to inspire confidence in kids.* We Are Teachers. https://www.weareteachers.com/growth-mindset/

Stace, C. (2021, February 25). *Five ways to build resilience in students.* Pearson International Schools. https://blog.pearsoninternational-schools.com/five-ways-to-build-resilience-in-students/

Steger, M. F., O'Donnell, M. B., & Morse, J. L. (2021). Helping students find their way to meaning: meaning and purpose in education. *The Palgrave Handbook of Positive Education,* 551–579. https://doi.org/10.1007/978-3-030-64537-3_22

Stærk, E. (2020, June 3). *Building kids' resilience through play is more crucial than ever.* Scientific American. https://blogs.scientificamerican.com/observations/building-kids-resilience-through-play-is-more-crucial-than-ever/

Suttie, J. (2017). *Four ways social support makes you more resilient.* Greater Good. https://greatergood.berkeley.edu/article/item/four_ways_social_support_makes_you_more_resilient

Sutton, J. (2020). *Erik Erikson's stages of psychosocial development explained.* Positive Psychology. https://positivepsychology.com/erikson-stages/

Teaching children to be resilient during times of adversity. (2020, October 14). University of Iowa Stead Family Children's Hospital. https://uihc.org/childrens/health-topics/teaching-children-be-resilient-during-times-adversity

The benefits of a growth mindset: learning from failure. (2019). Suncorp. https://www.suncorp.com.au/learn-about/teamgirls/growing-and-learning-from-failure.html

The brain architects: Building resilience through play. (n.d.). Center on the Developing Child at Harvard University. https://developingchild. harvard.edu/resources/podcast-resilience-play/

The do's & don'ts of teaching your child to cope. (2016, May 17). Psych Central. https://psychcentral.com/lib/the-dos-donts-of-teachin g-your-child-to-cope#1

The role problem solving skills play in raising a resilient child. (2020, September 15). Crawford International. https://www.crawford-international.co.za/the-role-problem-solving-skills-play-in-raisi ng-a-resilient-child

Three ways you can use social media to cultivate resilience. (n.d.). The Berkeley Well-Being Institute. https://www.berkeleywellbeing.com/thre e-ways-you-can-use-social-media-to-cultivate-resilience.html

Toole, B. (n.d.). *Risky play for children: Why we should let kids go outside and then get out of the way.* CBC. https://www.cbc.ca/natureofthings/ features/risky-play-for-children-why-we-should-let-kids-go-outsi de-and-then-get-out

Torregrossa Groves, T.M. (n.d.). *How resilience can combat the negative effects of cyberbullying: A workbook for parents and school counselors.* ProQuest. https://www.proquest.com/openview/629147eaddbd5f-315be85c68ceb5fcf9/1?pq-origsite=gscholar&cbl=18750&diss=y

Transforming the workforce for children birth through age 8: A unifying foundation. (n.d.). National Academies Press. https://nap.nationalacad-emies.org/read/19401/chapter/8

Tripple, M. (2021, May 5). *10 growth mindset activities for high school students.* Everything Mom. https://www.everythingmom.com/activities/ growth-mindset-activities

United Nations. (1989). *Convention on the rights of the child*. United Nations. https://www.ohchr.org/en/instruments-mechanisms/instruments/convention-rights-child

Upp, A. (n.d.). *3 ways I model resilience for my students*. Understood. https://www.understood.org/en/articles/3-ways-i-model-resilience-for-my-students

Vance, E. (2021, September 1). *The secret to raising a resilient kid*. The New York Times. https://www.nytimes.com/2021/09/01/parenting/raising-resilient-kids.html

Vogt, C. (2021, September 1). *Under pressure: Are the stresses of social media too much for teens and young adults?* Everyday Health. https://www.everydayhealth.com/emotional-health/under-pressure/are-the-stresses-of-social-media-too-much-for-teens-and-young-adults/

Wade, M., Wright, L., & Finegold, K. E. (2022). The effects of early life adversity on children's mental health and cognitive functioning. *Translational Psychiatry, 12(1).* https://doi.org/10.1038/s41398-022-02001-0

Wakeman, C. (2017, May 22). *Persistence vs. resilience: The difference matters*. Medium. https://medium.com/@CyWakeman/persistence-vs-resilience-the-difference-matters-7944bf83e2a4

Want to raise strong, resilient kids? Create "nurturing routines," says parenting expert—here's how. (2022, September 25). CNBC. https://www.cnbc.com/2022/09/24/how-to-raise-resilient-kids-by-developing-their-brains-with-nurturing-routines-parenting-expert.html

We all need help. Here's how to ask. (2021, May 17). Payne Resilience Training & Consulting. https://payneresilience.com/blog/2019/2/17/ask-for-help

What can schools do to build resilience in their students? (2013, October 30). Child Trends. https://www.childtrends.org/what-can-schools-do-to-build-resilience-in-their-students

Whitener, S. (n.d.). *The value of a growth mindset, and how to develop one.* Forbes. https://www.forbes.com/sites/forbescoachescouncil/2021/01/06/the-value-of-a-growth-mindset-and-how-to-develop-one/?sh=57a69b2a4d2f

Why a growth mindset is essential for learning. (2019, February 12). Learn to Code in 30 Days. https://learn.onemonth.com/why-a-growth-mindset-is-essential-for-learning/

Why children need creative problem-solving skills. (n.d.). National Inventors Hall of Fame. https://www.invent.org/blog/trends-stem/creative-problem-solving-skills

Why is problem solving important in child development? (2020, March 19). Marlborough. https://www.marlborough.org/news/~board/health-and-wellness/post/why-is-problem-solving-important-in-child-development

Wilcox, L., Larson, K., & Bartlett, R. (2021). The role of resilience in ethnic minority adolescent navigation of ecological adversity. *Journal of Child & Adolescent Trauma, 14.* https://doi.org/10.1007/s40653-020-00337-7

Wisner, W. (2022). *What are adverse childhood experiences (ACEs)?* Verywellmind.com. https://www.verywellmind.com/what-are-aces-adverse-childhood-experiences-5219030

Yacoub, A. (2021, September 30). *How to encourage a growth mindset in your child.* Therapy Works. https://therapyworks.com/blog/language-development/home-tips/growth-mindset/

Young, T. (n.d.). *Success and failure: How growth mindset can change education.* Mind Research Institute. https://blog.mindresearch.org/blog/how-growth-mindset-can-change-education

Zaera, A. (n.d.). *How to build resilience with video games.* Forbes. https://www.forbes.com/sites/forbeseq/2022/09/30/how-to-build-resilience-with-video-games/?sh=6a3976206a29

Zeng, S. (2021, August 30). *How social media can help cultivate more resilience.* Thrive Global. https://community.thriveglobal.com/how-social-media-can-help-cultivate-more-resilience/

Zimmerman, E. (2020, June 21). *What makes some people more resilient than others.* The New York Times. https://www.nytimes.com/2020/06/18/health/resilience-relationships-trauma.html

Made in United States
Troutdale, OR
12/07/2024

26039579R00113